GREAT LIVES IN BRIEF
A Series of Biographies

ACCURACY
BREVITY CLARITY
MULTUM
IN PARVO

These are
BORZOI BOOKS
Published by ALFRED A. KNOPF
in New York

NAPOLEON III

Napoleon III

A GREAT LIFE IN BRIEF

BY

Albert Guérard

New York   ALFRED A. KNOPF   1972

L. C. catalog card number: 55-5618

© ALBERT GUÉRARD, *1955*

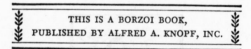
THIS IS A BORZOI BOOK,
PUBLISHED BY ALFRED A. KNOPF, INC.

PUBLISHED APRIL 11, 1955

FOURTH PRINTING, AUGUST 1972

NAPOLEON III

TO

MACLIN BOCOCK GUÉRARD

Merciless Critic

and

Beloved Daughter

Carlo Buonaparte (1746-1785)

Joseph	NAPOLEON	Lucien	Eliza
1768-1844	1769-1821	1775-1840	1777-1820
m. Josephine	m. (2) Marie-Louise		m. Prince
de Beauharnais	of Austria		Bacchioci
1763-1814	1791-1847		

(Stepchildren
of Napoleon)

Eugène	Hortense	Napoleon II,	Pierre
1781-1824	1783-1837	King of Rome,	1815-1881
		Duke of Reichstadt	
		1811-1832	

Roland
1858-1924

Princess George
of Greece

THE
BONAPARTE
FAMILY

A Condensed Genealogy

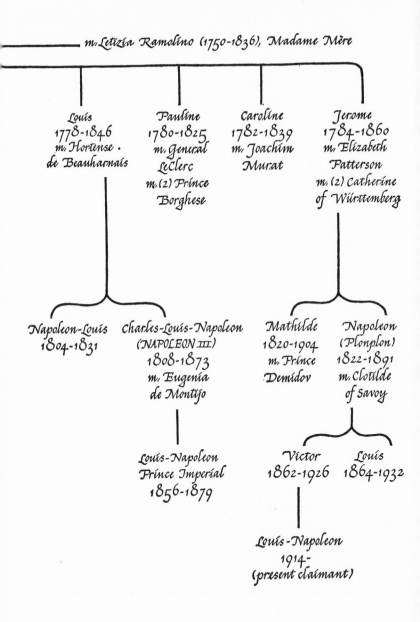

m. Letizia Ramolino (1750-1836), Madame Mère

Louis
1778-1846
m. Hortense
de Beauharnais

Pauline
1780-1825
m. General
LeClerc
m. (2) Prince
Borghese

Caroline
1782-1839
m. Joachim
Murat

Jerome
1784-1860
m. Elizabeth
Patterson
m. (2) Catherine
of Württemberg

Napoleon-Louis
1804-1831

Charles-Louis-Napoleon
(NAPOLEON III)
1808-1873
m. Eugenia
de Montijo

Mathilde
1820-1904
m. Prince
Demidov

Napoleon
(Plonplon)
1822-1891
m. Clotilde
of Savoy

Louis-Napoleon
Prince Imperial
1856-1879

Victor
1862-1926

Louis
1864-1932

Louis-Napoleon
1914-
(present claimant)

CHAPTER ONE

ON THE THRESHOLD
1808–1830

A GREAT life? The man whom Victor Hugo branded as *Napoleon the Little* had greatness thrust upon him: without the magic of his name, he would never have become, and have remained for twenty years, the master of France and the arbiter of Europe. Yet he was not merely, as his enemies called him, "Napoleon's cocked hat with no brains under it." He had to achieve greatness: an adolescent dream slowly matured, realized at last not through luck alone, but through pertinacity, shrewdness, and daring. The dream was not ignoble; indeed, it was more generous than the sheer love of personal power which impelled Napoleon I. There must have been greatness, however warped, in the man's very soul.

To his contemporaries, he was a mystery; to posterity, he remains an enigma. For thirty years after his downfall, his figure was veiled in a dark legend: all the iniquities of an insolent generation were heaped upon his head. In our own century, all reputable historians have striven to do him justice. But the traditional picture—the elderly rake, with waxed mustaches, heavy lids, and lackluster eyes, who swindled his way to the throne and collapsed at the stern touch of reality—that sinister caricature survives in popular imagination. After one hundred years, history still hesitates. His career, glittering and tragic, was a picaresque romance on an epic scale; but under the succession of sharply defined episodes, we find nothing but ambiguities at the core.

These ambiguities I shall not attempt to solve. I have
pondered over them from my first book to the present
one—a span of more than forty years. I have ventured
my guesses. Here my sole purpose will be to relate, as
simply as I can, what actually happened. The reader,
however, cannot shirk his responsibility. He must be
aware that a straight story cannot tell the whole story.
In a historical character we find a human being, with
all his confused yearnings and his pathetic flaws. But
we find also a symbol, the incarnation of collective
hopes and fears. Not only is the myth far more potent
than the man: paradoxically, it is also more definite.
Later ages will find Nazism a clear-cut entity, compared
with the turbid welter that was Hitler's mind. The Crusades, the Reformation, the French Revolution, are
more substantial than any crusader, reformer, or revolutionary. Communism dwarfs every communist. Like
a true epic, history on the proper scale depicts a com-
bat between gods: we may call them idols, we may
call them ideals. Had Napoleon III been Monsieur
Dupont, a private citizen, ambitious, unscrupulous, and
sensual, he might, after a couple of bankruptcies, have
climbed to a high position, amassed a fortune, married
a beauty, and died a broken man. Such a Monsieur
Dupont would bear a curious resemblance to the Napoleon we know; yet we are aware that he would not
be quite the same.

We shall descry, flitting in the background, vast
phantoms—Cæsarism, democracy, socialism, nationalities—which in fact were closer to the heart and soul of
Napoleon III than his accomplices Persigny and Morny.
We shall keep these abstractions in the background:
this is the story of a man, not an essay in political phi-

losophy. But a biography such as this cannot be severed from general history. For one moment at least, on December 10, 1848, the man and the France of his day were in unison. The clashing desires that swayed the country were his also. He was the Common Man or the Common Denominator. The moment was fleeting: soon Napoleon had to make a constant, groping effort to remain at the focal point. But the memory of that miraculous instant was not wholly effaced at the end of twenty-two years. In May 1870 the Emperor was not a tyrant ruling by force, and he was not a gilded figurehead. Precariously, fugitively, as we know, but impressively, he still was France. In his case, symbol and reality, biography and history, *almost* coincide. If we understand this one man, his time will become more intelligible.

His time, and our own. For the modern world begins in 1848, and the problems of that fateful year are still harassing us. In 1848 authority and liberty, democracy and socialism, nationalism and peace, science and religion, were tugging at men's minds even as they are today. The pamphlets and speeches of that era could be reprinted almost without a change and be used as weapons in our present controversies. This book is not a *Tract for the Times*. But if, incidentally, it compels the reader to question, purify, and thereby strengthen his own convictions, we shall return thanks to Napoleon III in his forgotten grave.

The one fixed star that guided Napoleon III's tortuous course was his belief in Cæsarian democracy: the will of the people, which is the will of God, incarnated in one man. This was expressed in the very title he was to assume: Emperor of the French by the Grace of God and the Will of the People. It was applied through his favorite institution, the plebiscite. It achieved the dignity of a doctrine in his youthful works, *Political Reveries, On Napoleonic Ideas*, and, at the summit of his career, in the Preface to his *Life of Cæsar*. Before we follow in plain sequence the events of that arresting and tormented existence, I should like to draw attention upon two episodes that focused the Cæsarian doctrine in his mind. They might be called his baptism and his confirmation in the Napoleonic faith.

The first occurred on June 1, 1815. Of the Hundred Days that Fate had allotted to the first Napoleon's last gamble, eighty had inexorably gone by. In a splendid ceremony, the new regime, the restored Empire, was to be solemnly proclaimed. Twenty thousand delegates, the Imperial Guard, the National Guard, deep masses from the capital, filled the vast sandy waste of the Champ-de-Mars. The strains of a *Te Deum* arose from an improvised altar. The results of the plebiscite confirming Napoleon on the throne were announced to the blare of martial music. New flags—the tricolor of Austerlitz, Jena, Wagram—were blessed by the clergy and presented to the regiments. When the Emperor asked the troops to swear allegiance to ruler and country, a formidable clamor arose and roared wave after wave: "We swear it!" It was a spectacle of undescribable grandeur, one of those mystic moments when it would seem that a whole people is conscious of a single soul. The Empress and the King of Rome were not present: Austria had claimed them as her own. But Queen Hortense, Napoleon's stepdaughter and sister-in-law, was there with her two sons. The younger, the future Napoleon III, was then just over seven years old, an age which, in the eyes of the Church, marks the beginning of responsibility. The child could not understand the misgivings and jealousies, the weary imperceptible shrugs, the despairing will-to-make-believe, the histrionics and the hysteria so apparent to a disenchanted observer like Fouché, who at that very moment was serving the Emperor only to betray him. For the sensitive boy, the scene must have been a revelation as though the heavens had opened: between the Napoleonic idea and the heart of France, a dark, profound, and indissoluble unity existed.

Sixteen years of obscurity followed. Louis-Napoleon is a young man of twenty-three. He has just escaped from the bullets of the Papal troops and the clutches of the Austrian police. Against the law that condemns his race to banishment, he is in Paris incognito, with his mother, Queen Hortense. The day is May 5, 1831, the tenth anniversary of the Emperor's death. From his window on the Place Vendôme, Louis-Napoleon watches—with what wild surmise!—the crowd flocking to the bronze column, trophy of his uncle's victories. The Parisians, so often accused of fickleness and levity, come reverently to the monument, as if to an altar. Once again Louis is made to feel the identity between the soul of the people and that of the martyred titan. Romantic nonsense, perhaps, but no less a poet than Victor Hugo was to voice it with religious fervor: "Napoleon, that god whose priest thou shalt be . . ." On the morrow, mother and son are notified by the police to leave the country. They comply; but the young prince remains stirred to the depths by this renewed sacrament. What if a sly and stodgy Citizen-King has

been whisked onto a shaky throne by a handful of journalists and financiers? Louis-Philippe has the money-
bags: the hearts are still Napoleon's. The young man's
faith is now indestructible. Twice he acts upon it, and
fails: he does not despair. On December 10, 1848 a
tidal wave makes him the ruler of France: he feels justified. For him the imperial idea was not a racket, as
Victor Hugo and Kinglake would have it: it was a
mission.

April 20, 1808, rue Cerutti (now Laffitte), in
Paris. In the early hours Her Majesty the Queen of
Holland had been delivered of a son. The birth was
premature and the child was frail: he had to be bathed
in wine and wrapped in cottonwool. But he was well
constituted, and survived to be Emperor of the French.

Imperial Paris showed proper elation: this was the
first Bonaparte to be born a prince. Napoleon, then
poised on the Spanish border, was overjoyed: he had
triumphal salvos fired all along the frontier. Without
legitimate issue of his own, he considered the sons of
his brother Louis as his destined heirs.

By 1808 the Empire had reached, not its fullest territorial extent, but the point of its greatest power and
glory. The Treaty of Tilsit had removed the Russian
menace. The consequences of the Berlin decree, closing the Continent to British commerce, were not yet
calamitous. Napoleon's worst blunders—his quarrel
with the Pope, his high-handed treatment of Spain—
were only in their incipient stage. For a brief season the
new Charlemagne seemed secure as Emperor of the
West.

In contrast with this splendor, the private life of the

imperial circle offered a mass of ill-smothered scandals and raucous squabbles. The hatred of the Bonaparte clan for the Empress Josephine and her brood reached the fierceness of a Corsican vendetta. They had disliked the intruder from the first: Napoleon's ardent devotion to her relegated them to a secondary position; her Old World graces made them look and feel like parvenus. They knew—the whole world knew—that she was flighty. Soon after the death of her first husband, General Alexandre de Beauharnais, guillotined "to encourage others," she had become one of the merry widows of the Thermidorian reaction. Barras was her close friend and protector: Barras, a Terrorist who had tripped Robespierre in self-defense, well aware that the Dictator of Virtue had a short way with profiteers; Barras, who, in that age of corruption, had attained a phosphorescent pre-eminence. It was with the blessing of Barras that the *grande dame* of an equivocal regime and the young Corsican adventurer were united. Even during the Italian campaign, their honeymoon barely over, Josephine was not above reproach. When Napoleon was away in Egypt, she made liberal use of her freedom. The Bonapartes in a body wanted the returning hero to cast her aside; and he would have done so but for the tears of his stepchildren, Eugène and Hortense de Beauharnais, whom he sincerely loved.

It was only then that Josephine began to appreciate the swarthy undersized husband, "Puss in Boots," whose passion she had at first accepted with amused tolerance. She mended her ways; only her incurable extravagance betrayed the whilom cocotte. She was nearing forty, and Creole beauties fade early. She knew that the Bonapartes had not disarmed; she attempted to pro-

tect herself and her children by means of a second connection with her husband's family. She had her way:
in 1802 her daughter, Hortense, married his brother
Louis.

The young pair was well assorted in age: he was
twenty-four, she nineteen. Both were great favorites
with the Master. Louis had been educated under the
eyes and at the expense of Napoleon. No light burden
on a lieutenant's pay: the elder brother had been forced
to deny himself every luxury. He felt well rewarded:
Louis, who followed him in Italy and Egypt, promised
to become an able and conscientious officer. Hortense,
after a checkered childhood, had gone through the fashionable school of Madame Campan, which was intended
to revive the delicate manners of the ancient regime.
She did not possess her mother's beauty, but she had
many accomplishments and a great deal of charm.

But this idyl in high places was deceptive. In Italy,
Louis had been stricken with that dread disease which
is one of the hazards of occupation forces; later his
troubles were ascribed, less convincingly, to rheumatism
contracted in Egypt. This vengeance of Venus profaned
was his ruin. All his life he remained a valetudinarian
and a hypochondriac, harassed with constant ailments,
obsessed with morbid fancies. On the other hand, Madame Campan's school had not smothered Hortense's
zest for life. Louis turned into a morose martinet; in the
words of Napoleon, he attempted to discipline his
sprightly young bride as he would drill a regiment.
There never was any deep love between them to alleviate
these tensions. Their hearts had been given elsewhere:
his to Émilie de Beauharnais, a niece of Josephine; hers
to Duroc, one of the most devoted lieutenants of Na-

poleon. Their union was what the French, with cruel irony, call a marriage of convenience.

The relentless Bonapartes took advantage of these un-happy circumstances. When a son was born to Louis and Hortense, the First Consul offered to adopt him as his heir; but his sister Caroline Murat spread the atro-cious slander that the child was in fact Napoleon's and had been conceived with the connivance of Josephine. A second son was born in 1804, but the incompati-bilities between the parents were not allayed.

In 1806 Napoleon decided to turn the Batavian Re-public, already a satellite of France, into a vassal King-dom of Holland under his brother Louis. Their royal honors brought no happiness to Louis and Hortense; indeed, they proved an added source of embitterment. Husband and wife adopted antagonistic policies. Louis made a commendable effort to become a good Dutch ruler and to protect the interests of his new subjects. Hortense remained a Frenchwoman at heart, and would never challenge the will of the Emperor. Their hostility became a public scandal. Louis drew up a formal treaty of peace, in eight articles, but after pious admonitions to forget and forgive, to love and to cherish, it sternly insisted upon full obedience on the Queen's part, and high-spirited Hortense refused to countersign her own subjection.

In 1807 their first child, the Prince Royal of Hol-land, died of croup. Grief brought the parents together at last. The Queen needed a change of scene, and found it in the Pyrenees, particularly at Cauterets. The King followed her and insisted upon a reconciliation, which was effected at Toulouse. But after a few weeks at the imperial court Louis desired to return to Holland, and

Hortense, pleading the state of her health, refused to follow him. She did eventually join her royal consort at Amsterdam; and even after his abdication they were to meet a few times. Their separation was formalized only many years later (March 8, 1815), not without bitter litigations. But after 1807 the breach between them was irremediable.

A shadow therefore hangs over the cradle of the child born on April 20, 1808. In spite of the Toulouse reconciliation, the enemies of Hortense cast doubts on his legitimacy. He might be the son of Admiral Ver Huel, a Dutch collaborationist who was to end his days as a Peer of the French Realm under Louis-Philippe; or perhaps of another Ver Huel; or of Charles Bylandt, Hortense's Dutch chamberlain; or of Decazes, a young magistrate who was attached to the cabinet of King Louis, and was to have a vertiginous ascent to the premiership and a dukedom under Louis XVIII. A letter from Louis to the Pope, in which he disclaimed fatherhood, is held to be a forgery, but many years later Prince Napoleon, son of Jerome, asserted that he had seen irrefutable documents to the same effect. In such a delicate matter we must be satisfied with the cautious Scots verdict: not proven. There was no physical resemblance between King Louis and his son the future Emperor. But the argument is not decisive: there was no resemblance either between King Louis and the other Bonapartes. On the other hand, the two surviving sons of Hortense were strikingly alike; and the legitimacy of the elder never was impugned. The attitude of King Louis himself was unequivocal: it was stern at times, but always fatherly. His letter sending his blessing to his son on the occasion of his first communion is solemn and touching. When the young prince got into bad scrapes, Louis disapproved, but interceded in his favor. He left him his entire fortune; and Louis was not the man to dissemble for three decades in order to spare the reputation of Queen Hortense.

At any rate, no suspicion seems to have entered the mind of Louis-Napoleon. He felt himself a Bonaparte through and through, both by blood and in the spirit. Alfred Neumann, in his inaccurate but very able romance *Another Cæsar*, holds that his passionate Napoleonic faith was a defense mechanism, a secret way of overcoming his own doubts as to his birth. The hypothesis is arresting, but it is not to be confused with history.

While Louis and Hortense were snarling at each other, the Empire was pursuing its splendid, disastrous course. In 1814, after a masterly but foredoomed campaign to defend France herself and his capital, Napoleon was forced to abdicate. Hortense had remained loyal to him—without illusions—as long as there was any hope. But when all was lost, she did not choose to cast her lot with the Bonapartes. Most decisively, she refused to obey her husband's command to follow him. In spite of their long association with the Republic and the Empire, the Beauharnais had their roots in the past: for them, the Bonapartes were prestigious upstarts. So Josephine, Eugène, Hortense, were ready to accept the change; and the Allies dealt very generously with them. Josephine entertained the Tsar. She lived but a few weeks, however, to enjoy the new turn of affairs. In the treacherous Parisian spring, she wore too diaphanous a dress at a reception for Alexander, caught cold, and died at La Malmaison on May 29. Eugène, who might have roused Italy, pledged his neutrality. Hortense obtained from the restored Bourbons the title of Duchesse de Saint-Leu, with a princely income. She duly waited on Louis XVIII to express her gratitude. Her frail, erratic bark had reached safety at last.

While the Congress was dancing in Vienna, Napoleon escaped from Elba. "The eagle, flying from steeple to steeple, came to rest on the towers of Notre-Dame." Hortense and her friends, Flahaut, Lavallette, Caulaincourt, were, she admits, "astonished and uneasy." All of them had served the Emperor loyally, but with their eyes open. They knew that his egomania was verging on madness. They were aware that, barring a miracle, the mad adventure must fail. And yet . . . They had seen miracles before. The very flight from Elba, the march on Paris with a handful of soldiers, the enthusiasm of the people: were these not miracles? Lafayette, the obstinate champion of freedom; Carnot, the republican Organizer of Victory; Lucien, who had steadfastly opposed the Empire and the Emperor; Benjamin Constant, friend and confidant of Madame de Staël—all these rallied to the new regime. Could the chastened conqueror learn the ways of liberty and peace?

We may add that the royalists had suspected Hortense of Bonapartist activities: when Napoleon's escape was announced, she had to hide from the Bourbon police. For these, and who knows for what other motives? she bravely turned her coat again and rallied to Napoleon. He received her coldly at first: he could not condone what he must call her treason of 1814. But he could not afford to be squeamish; he had to accept everyone ready to serve him, even Fouché. And he was fond of her as the daughter of Josephine and for her own sake. During the few weeks of that tremulous regime, Hortense almost filled the role of Empress by proxy.

I have alluded to the great ceremony at the Champ-de-Mars on June 1, the official proclamation of the renewed Empire. On June 12 Napoleon left Paris for Belgium. Ten days of intolerable suspense: salvos of artillery announced victories in which no one quite believed. Life went on, commonplace and unreal. On June 20 Benjamin Constant was reading to Hortense his short novel *Adolphe*, the most pitiless of all psychological dissections. All were in tears, even the cynical author. Then Savary, Duke of Rovigo, brought news of the disaster: on the 18th the army had been routed. On the 21st, at eight in the morning, Napoleon sneaked back into his capital.

The confused events of the next eight days are not part of our story. Napoleon, who abdicated for the second time on June 22, could have fought a political battle for his son's Empire or he could have fled; but, deserted by his "star," he seemed stricken with paralysis of the will. He retired from the Élysée to La Malmaison and bade Hortense join him. No romancer could devise a more poignant setting for those last days of freedom. La Malmaison had been his favorite country residence in the happy days of the Consulate. Summer was at its best; he and Hortense wandered in the delightful gardens in a sort of drugged, nostalgic peace. The wraith of Josephine still haunted the place. "My good Josephine, a woman through and through, the most charming person I have ever met!" "Ah, how sweet La Malmaison is! Surely, Hortense, we should be very happy if only we were allowed to remain here." On the 29th, Napoleon left for Rochefort, hoping to sail for America. He had waited too long, and he tarried unduly on the way. The trap was closing: on July 15 he surrendered to Captain Maitland on board H.M.S. *Bellerophon*.

Hortense's participation in the Hundred Days was to affect profoundly the career of her son. First of all, it made her an outcast and an exile: her coat could not be neatly turned a third time. She was thus committed, willy-nilly, to Napoleonism as she had never been before. Fond of romance as she was, she would give her political attitude a sentimental tinge: the last days at La Malmaison, so tragically sweet, effaced the stiffness, the coldness, at times the cruelty, from which she had suffered when the Emperor had been at the height of his power. Her Napoleon was the Napoleon of the Hundred Days—not the conqueror, not the despot, but the champion of the people's cause. "He, the Messiah of the people's interests, with his power, his strength of will, the prestige of his glory, he had called the nations to their share in the riches of this world, he had obtained for them their portion of earthly happiness. As Christ had rescued them from moral slavery, he had freed them from the bonds that prevented all but a privileged few from enjoying those positions and honors which, for centuries, certain classes had jealously preserved as their own. His imperial rule had firmly established the supremacy of merit over noble birth. . . . Was there any class in society, I asked myself, that had not benefited by his presence? Although his chief purpose had always been to uplift the masses . . . at the same time those rich and titled men who had plotted his downfall were also indebted to him for their very

lives, for having made peace between them and the
working classes, and for the sense of security and prosperity which resulted from such a peace." [1] These were
prophetic words. They gave a boldly distorted view of
Napoleon's actual rule, but they were in harmony with
the legend he was deliberately creating at that time in
St. Helena. *Napoleon the Messiah of the Masses:* in
that faith her son Louis was to live and die. It was Hortense who drew with a surprisingly firm hand the outline
of the Second Empire.

1815, which saw Hortense's political hopes shattered, also marked the devastation of her private life.
In March the final separation between her and Louis
was pronounced by the French courts, and Louis secured
custody of his elder son. But for the preceding five years
Hortense had considered herself morally free. She had
contracted with Count de Flahaut, a dashing officer
and the natural son of Talleyrand, a liaison that might
almost be called a morganatic marriage. The fruit of
that "open secret" affair was a certain "Demorny,"
whom, under a slightly improved name, we shall find
again in 1851, on the eve of the Coup d'État. Flahaut
was perhaps too handsome to be faithful; he certainly
was too shrewd to tie himself to a fallen queen. His
ardent flirtation with the great actress Mademoiselle
Mars was forgiven, but Hortense nobly released him,
so that he could marry into the high British aristocracy.
Henceforth Hortense adopted an elegiac attitude of
gentle and pious melancholy. Religion filled the void in
her heart; she filled her household with priests and

[1] *Mémoires de la Reine Hortense* (Paris, 1927), Vol. III,
pp. 48–9.

pined away—by imperceptible degrees—for twenty-two years.

Hortense had been ordered to leave Paris. Metternich provided her with an escort, Count Woyna. Woyna, "as handsome as a hero of romance," may have been assigned the same task with her as Neipperg had performed with Marie-Louise: Metternich was wily, and found uses for sirens of both sexes. But Flahaut was still in undisputed possession of Hortense's heart. Geneva refused to harbor her; Savoy discouraged her stay; Baden could provide only a temporary refuge. But her brother Eugène had become a loyal and much-appreciated Bavarian duke. Thanks to him, she was allowed to buy a house at Augsburg and a summer home at Arenenberg, in the Swiss canton of Thurgau. She traveled extensively, but Arenenberg was her fixed abode until her death, in 1837.

There, in that *gemütlich* Alamannic atmosphere, Louis-Napoleon grew to adolescence and young manhood: slow, affectionate, and gently stubborn. In spite of Hortense's new religiosity, the priest who had charge of his education was dismissed as too lax in his methods, and Philippe Lebas was appointed as his tutor (1820-7). A puzzling choice: Lebas was the son of a prominent Jacobin, one of Robespierre's inner circle, and he had remained faithful to his father's austere republicanism. He prescribed and enforced a rather formidable schedule. Fortunately, the boy's fondness for sports (he excelled in most) relieved the excessive tension. It is difficult to trace the extent of Lebas's influence: certain it is that Louis-Napoleon became neither a Jacobin nor a paragon of the sterner virtues. Lebas found his pupil docile, but not brilliant; the lad, in return, had more respect than affection for his mentor. Still, it was not indifferent that for seven years the prince should be associated with a man who had a sense of discipline and a conscience.

The frequent visits and voyages that Lebas deplored were in fact a much-needed corrective to his own pedantry. The elder son spent some time at Arenenberg, and the reunited brothers became fast friends. In exchange, Louis-Napoleon visited his father at Marienbad, Leghorn, and Florence. He also became intimate with his cousins in Munich and Baden. Especially, there were winters—1823, 1824, 1826—spent in Rome. Thanks to the generosity of the Holy See, Rome had become the rallying-point of the Bonapartes. Madame Letizia, Napoleon's mother; her half-brother Cardinal Fesch; Lucien, perhaps the ablest of them all, were permanent residents. The whole clan repeatedly gathered there.

But the most solid part of Louis-Napoleon's education came from the Gymnasium or high school at Augsburg. His record there was honorable: handicapped by his irregular training, he started near the bottom of the class, but his progress was steady. The influence of Augsburg was pervasive rather than dramatic; he seldom referred to it in later years, probably because he took it for granted. At any rate, although he spoke French at home, he became thoroughly Germanized in speech and thought. He was fonder of German poetry than of French; he was particularly steeped in Schiller, and, a prisoner after his lamentable failure at Boulogne, he found solace in translating *Die Ideale*. If His Smugness Albert the Good, Victoria's Prince Consort, and the slightly raffish Emperor of the French had a thoroughly good time together at Saint-Cloud, it was because they could swap old German songs and exchange students' memories. Albert's brother Ernest II, Duke of Saxe-

Coburg-Gotha, wrote: "Sometimes during a quiet chat, when he would sit in his armchair smoking cigarette after cigarette like a man in a dream, he gave me the impression of a German savant rather than of a sovereign of France. On such occasions he would recite whole poems by Schiller and would pass suddenly from French to German in his talk." Even in middle life Louis-Napoleon would show traces of a German accent. The opposition railed at him mercilessly on that score. Once, as we shall see, it served him well: the Assembly could not imagine that a man with such a thick Teutonic tongue could ever be dangerous in France. As Napoleon III he once congratulated Bismarck on his perfect French: "I have never heard a foreigner speak our language as you do." The future Iron Chancellor retorted: "Sire, I can return the compliment: I have never heard a Frenchman speak his language the way Your Majesty does." (When he spoke with deliberation, however, Napoleon III's French was not merely flawless; it was impressive.) It was said of Romain Rolland, so anxious to soar "above the strife," that "he spoke Swiss with a strong Esperanto accent." This gibe, in which there is a reluctant element of praise, could be applied to Louis-Napoleon. Of Corsican and Creole descent, a Dutch prince at birth, always an Italian at heart, a German in thought, thoroughly at home in British society, married to a Spaniard, he was far more European than French.

"War is the sport of kings"—no princely education is complete without at least the rudiments of military training. Many princes merely dabble at the martial game: Louis-Napoleon's schooling was modest but effective. He enlisted as a volunteer in the military academy at Thun, created and commanded by Colonel Guillaume-

Henri Dufour. Dufour was no bucolic warrior. He had gone through the great École Polytechnique in Paris, seen service as an engineer in Corfu, and won a captaincy in the French army during the Hundred Days. With him, at any rate, the Bonaparte name would be no handicap. For several summers the prince went through maneuvers. If he did not strike his fellow cadets as a genius (even at Magenta and Solferino, he was not an inspired leader), he commanded their respect for his willingness and his good humor. Like the family god, he was an artillerist. He was to write a creditable treatise on the subject, which he sent, with his compliments, to a number of French officers. Even in this technical field, uncle and nephew showed their radical divergences. Napoleon I was a virtuoso who made the best immediate use of available instruments, in this case the eighteenthcentury ordnance of Gribeauval. Napoleon III stumbled at times because he looked too far ahead: against a bureaucracy attached to the good old ways, he favored the breechloader, the Chassepot rifle, the machine gun. He retained his professional interest in artillery to the very end. In 1867, at the great Paris Exposition, he examined the steel cannon of Krupp with the attention of an expert. Incidentally, in the country of the fabulous marksman William Tell, he won prizes as a sharpshooter. All this is merely creditable: he never was a soldier at heart, while Napoleon I never was anything else. But when later he donned a French uniform, he was not a mere playactor.

The dynastic order imposed by the treaties of Vienna, so absurdly praised by some modern historians, did not last fifteen years. The first crack came with the rising of the Greeks against their Turkish masters in 1821. Eu

rope was already aglow with romanticism: here was a
movement at the same time national and religious, with
the fabled East as a background, and distant echoes of
the Crusades. Byron, the idol of the younger generation,
had espoused the Hellenic cause and died at Missolon-
ghi. Every generous soul was eager to fight. Russia, most
deeply interested in the conflict, remained hesitant. Re-
ligiously as well as politically, Turkey was the traditional
foe; the rivalry of the Christian powers was Islam's
strongest bulwark. Still, the Sublime Porte was part of
that *status quo* which it was Russia's mission to defend.
The Greeks were insurgents, rebels, subversives. They
stood for the freedom of a people: ominous words! The
dynasts could not make up their minds whether Navarino
was a glorious victory or an "untoward incident." Finally,
and with misgivings, Russia drifted into war.

Louis-Napoleon desired to fight the infidel under the
Russian flag: a noble cause to serve, experience to be
gained, prestige to be won; how stale and unprofitable
were the summer camps at Thun in comparison! Queen
Hortense herself was a romanticist. She had composed a
vapid Crusader's song, "Departing for Syria," which
became the French national anthem under the Second
Empire. She found it hard to resist her son's objurga-
tions: she gave a half-consent. In January 1829 Louis-
Napoleon asked his father's permission. King Louis, less
imaginative than his estranged wife, interposed his absolute veto. The young prince chafed, but obeyed.

This abortive but significant episode evokes a host of
companion pictures. The great Napoleon too had dreamt
of epic deeds in the gorgeous Orient. A quarter of a century later, in 1854, the would-be crusader found himself
at war with Russia and in alliance with the Turk. An-

other quarter of a century: another Louis-Napoleon, the Prince Imperial, was to seek experience and glory under a foreign flag and die in Zululand. Still another Louis-Napoleon, the grandson of King Jerome, was to become a general in the Russian service. History is a weird kaleidoscope.

We are compelled to note that, at an early age, the son of Hortense, the grandson of Josephine, sought other pleasures than reading Tacitus with Lebas, learning by heart the odes of Schiller, and drilling under Colonel Dufour. If chastity be virtue, Louis-Napoleon never was a virtuous man. In this respect neither the Bonapartes nor the Beauharnais were immaculate. The French have long shown great indulgence for the sins of Henri IV, Louis XIV, and even Louis XV; the British look with pride on the Nelson Column in Trafalgar Square without giving a thought to Lady Hamilton. Perhaps Robespierre alone could cast the first stone. In this chronicle, I shall not indulge in prurient gossip; neither shall I conceal or condone affairs which, involving the head of a state, were far from harmless.

We have reached the year 1829; the prince has just come of age; he is barely on the threshold of history. The picture we have of him at that time is nebulous. He is gentle, well-mannered, shy; yet, with young companions, he can be as mad as the rest. He is far from handsome: he had been a pretty child, and in middle life he achieved a style that is still remembered. But in his twenties and thirties his short stature—a long torso on top of inadequate legs—his nose already prominent, his scraggly mustache, made him, if not unprepossessing, at

least insignificant. There was a curious opacity in his eyes
of undefinable hue: what the world would later call
mystery then appeared only as dullness. His position was
no less indefinite than his appearance. Although the Napoleonic cult was spreading, there was no strongly organized Bonapartist movement. If there had been, he
could by no means have claimed to be its leader. He was
only fifth in line: the King of Rome was still alive; his
uncle Joseph, his father, Louis, had prior claims that
they had not formally renounced; he had a brother ahead
of him, more attractive than himself. Thus he was not
obviously marked by destiny. It would take a great upheaval and several accidents to give him his chance. It
would take also his unconquerable faith and his obscure
tortuous genius to turn a slender opportunity into a major
historical fact.

CHAPTER TWO

THE CONSPIRATOR
1830–1848

IN the summer of 1830 Louis-Napoleon was engaged as usual in his military training at Thun when he received news of the revolution in Paris. In "three glorious days," the capital had thrown off the Bourbons; and on the dome of the Tuileries the tricolor of the Republic and the Empire had replaced the white flag studded with golden lilies. The European order imposed by the Vienna settlement was tottering, and the Bonapartes, who had been its first victims, saw new vistas opening before them.

The clan gathered again in Rome in December 1830: Louis, Hortense, Jerome, and their children. Out of this family council came the firm decision to do nothing. The immediate heir of Napoleon, the King of Rome, was in the hands of Metternich. The former kings of Holland and Westphalia, never overbold, took a sober view of their own prestige. But if the middle-aged Bonapartes were realistic, those of the new generation were thrilled with hopes. The two sons of Louis, and their cousins— Jerome's elder son, barely sixteen, and Pierre, son of Lucien, even younger—dreamed of a sensational stroke. As a start, they would simply capture the Vatican. Plot or prank, the madcap adventure was frustrated. The adolescents, Jerome and Pierre, were quietly restrained. The elder princes, who ought to have known better, were allowed to slip away. The whole plan was preposterous unless the young men had actually joined the

Carbonari and were expecting their support. This has
not been proved beyond cavil. At any rate, they were in
sympathy with the aims of that secret order: the liberation of the peoples, and, first of all, of Italy.

In February 1831 an insurrection broke out in Romagna, the northern province of the Papal States. In
Florence, Menotti, a noted Italian patriot, had already
approached the princes. With a high sense of filial duty,
they refrained from consulting their parents, so as not to
have to disobey them, and joined the rebels. They were
hailed with enthusiasm and given responsible commands:
there was magic in the Napoleonic name.

The young men, twenty-seven and twenty-three, enjoyed themselves hugely, and did well at first with the
little army of from three thousand to five thousand men.
The elder repelled a body of Papal troops. The younger
was preparing with coolness and skill for an assault on
Civita Castellana which might have opened the road to
Rome. There it was that Count Felice Orsini died in
the ranks of the revolutionists. Twenty-seven years later
his son was to remind Napoleon III of his duty to Italy
by hurling a bomb at him: "He missed his body and
reached his soul."

A victory over the pontifical troops was not out of the
question. But the skirmishes in Romagna were minor
incidents on the European scene. The insurgents had
hoped that the new France, the France of the Tricolor,
would come to their support. On the contrary, the very
presence of the Napoleonic princes gave the new King,
Louis-Philippe, an excellent excuse for not intervening.
So the young men were told by the revolutionary government at Bologna that their services had become embarrassing. Bitterly humiliated, they retired to Forlì.

There the elder died on March 17 after a three-day bout with a pernicious fever. Such, at any rate, was the official version. If, as others chose to believe, he had been shot by a malcontent, perhaps by a rival, there seems no reason why the story should have been kept a secret.

Hortense, who in the whole affair showed admirable devotion and energy, had rushed to the help of her sons. The Vatican might have treated them with paternal leniency, but the Austrians had now entered upon the scene, and they had decreed death against all foreign volunteers. Hortense had great difficulties in tracing the princes. When they were located at last, she found one dead and the other stricken with measles—no light disease in an adult. All frontiers were closed to the outlaws. Hortense fooled the Austrians into believing that she had already sailed for Corfu, while, with forged papers, she remained at Ancona. Fate, fond at times of old-fashioned, well-contrived plots, would have it that the Austrian official in command should pick out for his residence the very palazzo in which she was hiding her son. She pretended to be sick, was allowed to retain a few rooms, managed to keep the invalid invisible and inaudible, and nursed him into convalescence. Early on Easter morning, under pretext of hearing Mass at Loretto, she moved out, with the prince in the character of a valet. To pass from the Papal States into Tuscany and from Tuscany, through Massa and Genoa, into France, required the Queen's utmost resourcefulness. The law exiling the Bonapartes from France had not been repealed, but it had lost its moral force with the downfall of the Bourbons. So mother and son proceeded unhampered to Paris, with definite hopes of a favorable arrangement with King Louis-Philippe.

Louis-Philippe did receive Hortense with courtesy
and kindliness, but under conditions of extreme secrecy.
The King was in a quandary; indeed, he was to spend
the eighteen years of his reign in a quandary. It is un-
comfortable to be, not the representative of a clear-cut
principle, but, avowedly, a compromise, a stopgap, a
makeshift. He was a royal prince and "the best of republicans"; ruler by the grace of the barricades and the
defender of order; King of the French—or at least of the
happy few who were the heaviest taxpayers. He was,
and knew it only too well, the most experienced, the
shrewdest of French politicians, and he was assigned the
role of a mere figurehead.

The Citizen-King was humane. He had tasted the
bitterness of exile, and he did not want to inflict it upon
adversaries. He had no prejudice against the Bonapartes.
He had already started capitalizing on the Napoleonic
legend, rife throughout France and Europe. He was sur-
rounding himself with survivors of the Empire, "illustrious swords" like Marshal Soult, decorative civil servants
like Maret, Duke of Bassano, and Savary, Duke of Rovigo. In 1840 he was to stage most successfully the grand
pageant of Napoleon's second burial, "the Return of the
Ashes." This was not sheer Machiavellism. He was conscious that the Napoleonic regime and his own, antip-
odal as they seemed, had a deep purpose in common:
to reconcile with the principles of 1789 the stability attached to the monarchical tradition. It would therefore
have suited his book to grace his court with the Emperor's family; and Hortense was ready to play her part.
But . . .

Metternich held the trump card: the Duke of Reichstadt, Napoleon II. But Napoleonic sentiment at that

time had assumed a democratic tinge: could not a Republican-Bonapartist coalition upset Louis-Philippe's wobbly throne? So the King remained noncommittal: "Sometime, perhaps, but not yet." And he ordered Hortense and Louis out of the kingdom. Pleading Louis's state of health, they lingered; and the King was informed that the young prince was meeting republican leaders. It was then, on May 5, that Louis saw Parisian crowds, with unwonted reverence, fill the Place Vendôme. The precarious equilibrium that Louis-Philippe was attempting to maintain could be upset at any moment. So the royal police became peremptory: Hortense and Louis had to leave at once.

They went to England, and stayed there, mostly in London, for about three months, officially ignored, privately well received. By the end of August 1831 they were again at Arenenberg. Louis had barely reached that haven when a delegation of Polish patriots urged him to lead their insurrection. A flattering tribute to his importance, but he had just been scalded, and he sensibly declined the honor. He was well advised, for on September 8 "order reigned in Warsaw." For the next five years he was to be more Swiss than ever.

At any rate, he turned into a model Swiss. He wrote a serious treatise: *Political and Military Considerations on Switzerland*, which was favorably received. He was granted civil rights in the canton of Thurgau, and was made an honorary citizen of the republic. In 1834, the canton of Berne made him a captain of artillery; and his *Artillery Manual* was highly commended by the great Dufour. This quiet Swiss period is often overlooked. It proved at least that Louis was no mere gambler. Nor did he rely blindly on the "star" of his race. Very different

from the Legitimist pretender, he was a fatalist who believed that Providence demands our active co-operation.
Constantly we shall find in him the alternation, the co-
existence, of a bold imagination, of a secretiveness that
looked like apathy, but with no lack of conscientious
practical work.

In the meantime his position in the Bonapartist world
had greatly changed. His elder brother was dead. Now
his cousin, Napoleon II, the Duke of Reichstadt, died
on July 22, 1832, to remain buried, a Habsburg prince,
in the crypt of the Capuchin Church in Vienna until
Adolf Hitler chose to return his remains to France. At a
family council held in London in 1832, it was made evident that his uncle Joseph and his father, Louis, would
never move a finger to assert their claims. So Louis-
Napoleon could feel himself, in spirit and in fact, although not yet according to the letter of the law, the sole
representative of all imperial hopes.

In 1835 there came to him, with a letter of introduction from King Joseph, a fiery young journalist of
his own age, Victor Fialin, self-styled Viscount de Persigny. Persigny was a character out of Balzac: Rastignac,
Vautrin, Philippe Bridau, would have acknowledged the
kinship. Having joined the army, he had reached non-
commissioned rank in the hussars when the stormy days
of 1830 made him dissatisfied with his humdrum military existence. His revolutionary attitude led to his being
discharged, and he became a very minor journalist in
Paris. He seems to have flirted with the Legitimists, but
he was caught in all sincerity by the romantic wave of
Napoleonic sentiment. He was an adventurer, no doubt;
his political intelligence was none too subtle; his energy
was mostly bluster; but he was filled with a single pur-

pose, and he remained obstinately loyal to his Bonapartist ideal. It is difficult to appraise his influence on
Louis. I am inclined to believe that the pretender did
not need so coarse an instrument. Persigny was to follow
Napoleon for nearly forty years, a devoted, ambiguous,
slightly sinister shadow; and the Emperor was to pay
him a double-edged tribute: "Among all the people
around me, there is but one true Bonapartist—Persigny—*and he is mad.*"

On the evening of October 31, 1836 the "aerial telegraph" brought to the Tuileries this puzzling message
from Strasbourg: "This morning October 30 about six,
Louis-Napoleon, son of the Duchesse de Saint-Leu, *who
had in his confidence* Colonel Vaudrey of the Artillery,
went through the streets of Strasbourg with . . ." This
aerial telegraph was an elaborate semaphor system devised by Claude Chappe in 1792. In fair weather it
cut the transmission of dispatches from days to minutes.
But this was late autumn; a fog arose, blurred the part
italicized, and obliterated the end.

Guizot, the ablest statesman of the reign, has left us
a sober, dignified, yet profoundly dramatic account of
that night of suspense. The men who gathered at the
Tuileries had served many regimes; they had no deep
faith in the Orleanist compromise. They eyed one another with misgivings and wondered whether their coats
could stand being turned once more. Morning brought
relief: the alarm was over, the prince a prisoner.

It was a near thing, as Wellington said at Waterloo.
The plot had been well contrived. There were demo-
cratic and Napoleonic sympathies in Strasbourg. Colonel
Vaudrey, at the head of two artillery regiments, had been

won over. Fialin de Persigny had provided, among other
arguments, a vivid siren, Eleonore Gordon, *née* Brault,
swordswoman and concert singer, whom the gallant
colonel found irresistible. General Voirol, commanding
the garrison, had not committed himself, but was understood to be a sympathizer. The first moves went according to plan. The prince met the assembled regiments in
the dimness of early dawn; he addressed them and placed
himself at their head, and they followed him. Whither?
Did he himself know, or did he trust to the inspiration
of the moment? There was some fumbling, some delay.
Voirol, hastily aroused, stopped the show. Louis wanted
no bloodshed; he and his accomplices were arrested without a fight. Persigny alone managed to escape.

All then was for the best in the best of bourgeois
monarchies; but Louis-Philippe, when Voirol's reassuring message reached him at last, may have cast a quiz-
zical glance at his courtiers. He affected to consider the
plot as a mere extravaganza. He shipped the young hot-
head on the frigate *Andromède*: she was to cruise slowly
as far as Brazil, then turn north and drop the prince
where adventurers rightly belonged, in the United States.
The King even gave him 15,000 francs (about
$3,000) as pocket money, a surprising gesture on the
part of so thrifty a monarch; but 200,000 francs had
been found on the prince, and duly confiscated, so the
royal exchequer was not the loser.

Through a strange blunder, the government prose-
cuted the accomplices after pardoning the chief character.
The result was disastrous for the regime. Although the
accused struck a defiant attitude, they were acquitted by
a Strasbourg jury, and the whole city rejoiced in the
verdict. A hastily scribbled biography of the pretender

sold by the thousands. Louis had gained in stature by this abortive attempt. Charged to the advertising account, his money had not been spent in vain.

On March 30, 1837 Louis landed at Norfolk, Virginia, and proceeded to New York. He had hoped for letters of introduction from his uncle Joseph, who had spent years in America as Count de Survilliers. The nominal head of the family snubbed him, but Louis was already a celebrity in his own right. He was lionized in New York by society and the literary world. Some thought him "as mad as a March hare" because he would say with perfect gravity: "When I am Emperor of the French . . ." But he was writing observations on America which were singularly sensible, and at times prophetic. He was planning extensive travels in the country, if not permanent residence, when he received news of his mother's severe illness. He hurried to her bedside. In spite of the obstacles placed in his path by the French government, he reached Arenenberg on August 4 and was with Hortense until the end, on October 9. In their checkered and at times questionable lives, their mutual devotion had been the one fixed star.

The prince had accepted deportation, but he had given no pledges in exchange for leniency. Louis-Philippe, however, chose to consider his return to Europe as a breach of faith, and he brought pressure to bear upon Switzerland to expel his political enemy. Count Molé, who, like all weak men, was not averse to safe bullying, massed troops on the frontier. Louis, as we have seen, had behaved admirably as a guest of Switzerland, and had in fact become an adopted son. The Swiss, jealous of their independence, proud of their traditional hospitality, refused to be cowed by Molé's bluster. While the federal government delayed its reply, canton after canton pronounced itself in favor of Louis-Napoleon. The Swiss could indulge in that heroic attitude with a comfortable mixture of righteousness and security: they had been assured that the prince intended to leave of his own accord. He went over to England: the wrath of Louis-Philippe could threaten to cross the Jura, but not the Channel. The conflict had greatly enhanced the importance of Louis-Napoleon throughout Europe: *The Times* made constant references to him in its weighty editorials.

For nearly two years Louis-Napoleon moved with surprising ease in the best circles of London society. Exclusive clubs, mansions, and country houses were generously opened to him. His name and his adventures had made him a celebrity. His being *persona non grata* with Louis-Philippe was a strong point in his favor, for the *Entente cordiale* of those days had reached its most acrimonious stage. He was affluent with Hortense's inheritance; his dinners and his stable were beyond praise; his breeding was faultless; he was an excellent shot; and he sat his horse well. He offered then, as he did on the throne, a mystifying combination of flamboyancy and restraint. If in August 1839 he was one of the Knights in the fabulous Eglinton Tournament, an elaborate and ruinous medieval pageant that evoked not a little criticism, men of British blood bore a much heavier responsibility. If his taste in waistcoats was a trifle florid, this was no damning offense in the days of Count d'Orsay, Bulwer Lytton, and Disraeli. In small things as well as in great, the future Earl of Beaconsfield and the future Emperor of the French were kindred spirits. Both had in them more than a dash of the adventurer; both had powers of bold and constructive statesmanship. In 1880 Disraeli, in his last romance, *Endymion,* was to describe "Prince Florestan" in Carlton Terrace with genuine admiration and sympathy.

Louis-Napoleon's display of his imperial pretensions met with courteous reticence. No one took it amiss that his carriage should be emblazoned with imperial arms, or that he appeared at the opera with two aides-de-camp in attendance. He could manage to be the reverse of unassuming in the quietest, most gentlemanly manner. These happy months in England were to bear fruit. His city-planning was inspired in part by the London squares. It was in England that he acquired the sense of the industrial age. And it became a cardinal principle of his policy to remain on friendly terms with England.

At this point two echoes of *chronique scandaleuse* may find their place in our history. The first is a mere episode, an absurd duel with an absurd personage. Napoleon I, wanting to establish that he could procreate children, had performed a scientific experiment with meticulous care. The chosen laboratory was Eleonore Denuelle de la Plaigne, a school friend of Caroline Murat; the result was Count Léon. Léon, like his half-brother Walewski, and unlike the King of Rome, was the living image of his imperial father. His feelings may be imagined when he saw a mere nephew, and a dubious one at that, pose as the legitimate heir while he, Napoleon's undoubted flesh and blood, was naught but an eccentric and disreputable gambler. He went to London with the express purpose of challenging his "little cousin," and the prince consented to a duel. The would-be fighters fussed so long over the choice of weapons that they gave

the slow-footed British police time to intervene. The affair attracted little attention and was soon forgotten. Léon
attempted to play a political part in 1848, as did several
of his recognized cousins. Although the Second Empire
had no prejudice against the bar sinister, Léon was kept
out of court circles. He died obscurely in 1881.

Far more significant was Louis-Napoleon's connection
with Miss Elizabeth Ann Haryett, who had assumed the
name of Miss Howard. She was a lady of determination,
charm, and wealth; how that wealth had been acquired
need not be investigated. She was not merely Louis-
Napoleon's mistress: she became one of the most ardent
and most generous of his supporters, and we shall find
her again in December 1851. Incidentally, she may
have been the cause of Kinglake's damaging account of
the *Coup d'État*, in his monumental and spirited *Invasion of the Crimea*: fifteen years before, the historian had
been the unsuccessful rival of the pretender. "*Et c'est
ainsi qu'on écrit l'histoire.*"

But the greatest event in those two very active years
was the publication, in 1839, of *Des idées napoléoni-
ennes.* In this book, the earlier *Rêveries politiques*
(1832) were brought into sharper focus. Cæsarian democracy assumed the dignity of a doctrine and the defi-
niteness of a manifesto. To understand its full impact, we
must remember the dismal squabbles among the parliamentary oligarchs of the July monarchy. Louis-Napoleon's message was a call to greatness and decision. The
response was gratifying. Lamartine, an anti-Bonapartist
himself, speaks of its running to 500,000 copies. This
is no doubt a romantic exaggeration, but the book did
find a vast audience.

.   .   .

There had so far been so much method in Louis-Napoleon's madness that the next move comes as a sharp surprise. The Strasbourg venture, though it failed, had not been ludicrous. In the four years that followed, the pretender seemed to have grown in experience, dignity, and intellectual maturity. Yet we now find him engaged in an enterprise that looks like a clumsy farce. It is one of the many enigmas in that mysterious career.

At nine o'clock in the morning on August 4, 1840, the small steamer *Edinburgh Castle*, chartered for a month, left the wharf at London Bridge, ostensibly for a pleasure cruise. Members of the "party" were picked up at Greenwich, Gravesend, Margate, and Ramsgate, which last was not reached until dawn on the following day. Landing at Boulogne by daylight would have greatly added to the risk; remaining in harbor might have aroused suspicion. So the *Edinburgh Castle* put out again and cruised aimlessly all day long. Many readers may have had unpleasant experiences of the Channel when it was smooth: on that day it was rough. The new Argonauts fought seasickness with alcohol. Their condition may be imagined when they reached Wimereux, some three miles north of Boulogne, shortly after midnight. But their valor was adequate to the kind of fighting they would have to face.

Among the fifty-six members of the expedition, the majority were Frenchmen; a few were Poles. Some were personal servants of the prince; the rest had been recruited at a hundred francs a head in the "Little Alsatia" of Soho. They were issued uniforms with the regimental number 40. When told of the enterprise ahead, they cheered. It might turn into an epic; at any rate, it was a lark.

To cap the absurdity, rumor (echoed three decades later by Rochefort and Gambetta) had it that a tame eagle was to hover over the prince's head, attracted by a strip of bacon concealed in his Napoleonic hat. History admits that there was a queer bird in the affair: some say a vulture, the pet of the sea captain. As there was only one boat, landing the little troop was a long process. A pair of coast guards were put off with a cock-and-bull story; and the expeditionary force was duly met by the prince's accomplice, Lieutenant Aladenize, of the 42nd.

Thus the brave company marched to the regimental barracks in the lower part of Boulogne. Thanks to the presence of Aladenize, the sentry post presented arms. In the yard, Louis-Napoleon granted promotions to a few deserving veterans, while silver coins were thrown to the small crowd that had gathered outside. So civilians as well as military took up the cry: *"Vive l'Empereur!"* The affair was unrolling pleasantly enough when, as at Strasbourg, the commanding officer, hastily buttoning his tunic, burst upon the scene. It was Captain Col-Puygelier. Persigny would have killed him, but was restrained by Aladenize. In the scuffle, the pretender fired a pistol and wounded a soldier. Col-Puygelier had little trouble in rallying his men. Still, he allowed the invaders to retire, and simply locked the gates after them.

It was six in the morning. Instead of retiring to the beach after the obvious failure of this commando raid, Louis-Napoleon went to the upper town within its old-world ramparts and attempted to force a gate. Unable to break through, he led his little troop to the Column of the Grand Army, commemorating the immense prepa-rations made in 1805 for a descent on the English coast. As a final gesture, the imperial flag was planted atop. Meanwhile, most of the fifty-six had fled, only to fall singly into the hands of the regulars and of the National Guards. The faithful remnant tried to reach an empty lifeboat. A volley was fired at them: one was shot dead, another drowned, the prince himself wounded. The boat capsized, and the soaking greatly impaired the dignity of the Emperor's nephew. In that bedraggled condition he was jailed in Boulogne Castle. Soon he was taken over to the fortress of Ham in Picardy.

Such an abject failure, I repeat, was not in character, for Louis-Napoleon in 1840 was a very different personage from Hitler at the time of the *Bierhalle Putsch* in Munich. Two explanations could be advanced. The first is that Louis-Napoleon was relying on support that did not materialize. Among the men whom his agents approached was General Magnan, in command at Lille. After the fiasco, Magnan swore that he had indignantly rejected the offers. Some thought that he protested too much. The Prince did not betray any of his accomplices. But in 1851, at the time of the *Coup d'État*, Magnan was placed at the head of the army in Paris. Cautious even in this rash venture, he refused to act except upon definite orders from his superior, the Minister of War. But act he did, and his services were rewarded with a marshal's baton. Had Col-Puygelier lost his nerve, the Army of the North, under Magnan, might have been found ready to follow the pretender's eagles. Conversely, had a Col-Puygelier been on hand at Cannes in March 1815, France and Europe might have been spared the costly episode of the Hundred Days. If Magnan or

others had given a nod or a wink that a Bonapartist agent
could misinterpret as approval, it would have left no
trace in history.

Imponderables may be weightier than documented
facts: that is why history can never be scientific in exactly
the same manner as chemistry. In this instance the mighti-
est of imponderables was the Napoleonic Legend. Thiers,
the devoted historian of the Consulate and the Empire,
Prime Minister in 1840, whipped up Napoleonic
memories so as to revive the spirits of France in a severe
diplomatic crisis. Louis-Philippe, after Thiers's policy
had led to a humiliating setback, fostered the Legend
with might and main as a glittering mask for his own
drab and sensible attitude of peace-at-any-price. So the
chronology of this crucial year 1840 is instructive. On
May 12 the Chambers decreed the return of Napoleon's
remains from St. Helena. On August 5 Louis-Napoleon
made his attempt at Boulogne. On October 6 he was
sentenced by the Chamber of Peers. On October 16
Napoleon's body was taken aboard the French frigate
quaintly named *The Beautiful Chicken* (*La Belle
Poule*), under command of Joinville, "the Sailor Prince,"
third son of Louis-Philippe. On December 15, with
perhaps the most impressive ceremonies in the long annals of France, the Emperor's body was laid down at
the Hôtel des Invalides, according to his wishes, "on
the banks of the Seine, amid that French people he had
loved so well." And on August 15, 1841 a bronze
statue was placed on that very Column of the Grande
Armée at Boulogne at which, almost exactly a year before, the nephew's bid for power had come to such a
sorry end.

Louis-Napoleon's error, shared by many historians to

the present day, was to take the Legend far too seriously. It was, to a large extent, make-believe; and Thackeray, who witnessed "the Second Funeral," had some justification for his ironical account of the affair. France, like all other countries, is both Don Quixote and Sancho Panza. As Ximénès Doudan put it so well, the French bourgeois is eager to "bestrew with his corpse" all the battlefields of Europe while toasting his toes by his cozy fireside. This duality was perfectly understood by shrewd Louis-Philippe, whose secret motto was: "France's business is Business." So on December 15, 1840 the royal family was hailed with deafening applause while few gave even a passing thought to the Emperor's heir, a prisoner for life. This demonstrates as neatly as anything can be demonstrated in history that the future rise of Louis-Napoleon was not owing *entirely* to the Legend. For 1840 saw both the zenith of the Legend as a romantic myth and the nadir of Bonapartism as a political reality.

After what seemed an ignominious fall, Louis-Napoleon, undaunted, started dreaming and working again. First of all, he used his trial to excellent purpose. He did not appeal for mercy or even for leniency: his defense was a challenge. Louis-Philippe was aware that he could not trust a common jury; so he had the conspirators brought before the Chamber of Peers as a high court of political justice. Many of the peers had started their careers under the Empire. Out of 312 members, only 152 voted the final condemnation. Count de Flahaut and Admiral Ver Huel very properly excused themselves.

Louis-Napoleon had a case. He was no mere agitator: he stood for a principle. And that principle was the very foundation of democracy: government by con-sent of the governed. France, in his eyes, had created and ratified the power of Napoleon through a series of pleb-iscites in 1800, 1802, 1804, 1815; and had deposed him only through the force of foreign bayonets. Louis-Philippe on the contrary had been called to the throne by a small cabal and endorsed by a rump plutocratic Parliament. Louis-Napoleon had come, not to assert his own dynastic claims, but to demand that the people be consulted.

These principles he stated with singular force, for he could at times reach eloquence. It was no mere chance that Berryer had consented to be his counsel. Berryer, the greatest orator of the time, was a Legitimist. He too had never ceased to consider the Orléans as usurpers. A government should rule by the grace of God, as did the Bourbons of the elder branch. In default of that blessing, it could derive from the will of the people a kind of pragmatic legitimacy. Louis-Philippe could ad-vance neither claim.

But the peers who voted, and even those who ab-stained, were hand-picked profiteers and servitors of the regime. So their verdict was inevitable. Louis-Napoleon was sentenced to perpetual incarceration in a fortress. With his enigmatic smile, he queried: "How long is perpetual?" There was no popular revulsion of feeling in his favor: as we noted, no shadow fell on the great pageant of December 15. Yet his condemnation was no moral victory for the Bourgeois King.

Ham was a dismal fortress in the swampy upper reaches of the river Somme, sixty miles or so north of

Paris. Modern alterations had ruined its medieval pictur-
esqueness without adding to its comforts. It was damaged
beyond repair during the First World War. Louis-
Philippe was not vindictive; above all, he was too sensible to turn another Napoleon into a martyr. The prince
was given a fairly commodious apartment: a large study
in a round tower, with a small bedroom attached. Damp-
ness had made these quarters unsightly, but this was soon
remedied. Louis-Napoleon had with him two of his
most faithful followers: Conneau, Hortense's doctor, a
dear family friend who never abandoned him; and General de Montholon, who had closed the Emperor's eyes
in St. Helena. He had also his personal servants, in particular his confidential valet, Thélin. He had a garden,
and he was allowed to ride along the ramparts. The material conditions, including the climate, were actually
worse than at St. Helena, where Napoleon I had been
allowed to keep a veritable little court. But the spirit
was different; perhaps because Louis was not disposed,
like his uncle, to make capital out of petty grievances;
perhaps because prisoners and turnkeys were all of them
French; above all, because Demarle, the commanding
officer, was no Sir Hudson Lowe. It is pleasing to think
of the chief warden and his charges chatting over a
friendly hand of whist under the soft light of an oil
lamp.

Louis was not denied other satisfactions, which, from
early youth to premature old age, his temperament
seemed to require. Women were allowed to visit him.
One, blooming and prompt to laughter, took away and
brought back his laundry. She was known as *La Belle
Sabotière*, the fair daughter of the clogmaker. Her two
sons received estates and titles under the Second Empire,

and must have ended their days as honored country squires. History knows them no more.

Louis accommodated himself to the routine of his cap-tivity. It affected his health: he was to show long traces of anemia. But it failed to break his spirit. On the con-trary, it gave him a chance to complete his education. Those six studious years were for him, as he liked to put it, "the University of Ham." People were astounded later at the range and seriousness of his information: the Duke of Saxe-Coburg-Gotha noted that there was in him something of a German savant. He sent letters and occasional articles to many newspapers, "on all things knowable, and a few others besides." He composed a pamphlet on the proposed Nicaragua Canal; in later years he was a great promoter of public works, and it was thanks to his support that Lesseps was able to create the Suez Canal. He had previously reached definite con-clusions on political principles; so he went on to social problems. As a Cæsarian democrat, he was concerned with the interests of the common people; so he became, without any affiliation to any particular school, a socialist in the spirit. The Second Empire, under his guidance, was to have a Saint-Simonian tinge, technocracy with a faint religious aura.

Above all, he was in close touch with the thought of Louis Blanc. They corresponded; Louis Blanc went to visit him and was astounded to find in him such an apt disciple. Karl Marx has made it the fashion to brand all socialists before him as "utopians." The name does not fit Louis Blanc any more than it fits Robert Owen. Blanc, an excellent historian and a competent politician, had very definite and very practical ideas. He realized that the bourgeoisie of the Louis-Philippe era was too

selfish and too timorous to understand the industrial revolution. So he conceived of large-scale enterprise pro-
moted, owned, and managed by the state: this is what
he meant by National Workshops. Louis-Napoleon's
short book *On the Extinction of Pauperism* is true to the
Louis Blanc spirit, without seeking to supplant the capitalistic system. His "reserve army of labor" was some-
what akin to the CCC and the PWA of the New Deal,
as well as to the EPIC plan of Upton Sinclair. The book
had a wide circulation. Again, if Louis had been just
Monsieur Dupont or Monsieur Durand, his position
among social planners would not be an outstanding one.
But he was a pretender. The contrast was glaring between the sweep and generosity of his thought and the
purblind petty *realism* of the Louis-Philippe world.

King Louis was living in Florence, a lonely and bitter man. His health, long precarious, was fast breaking
down. He had taken spasmodic interest in his only surviving son. Now he approached Louis-Philippe's government with a request for Louis-Napoleon's release.
The prince himself, on Christmas Day 1845, wrote to
the Minister of the Interior, and, on January 14, 1846,
directly to the King. He pledged his word that he would
return to prison as soon as he had performed his filial
duties. The French government wanted more: the formal
abandonment of his claims. These claims were his religion: no compromise could be found. Thereupon Louis-
Napoleon made up his mind to escape.

He might have had chances before, and he probably
had accomplices within his jail. But there is no proof
that Louis-Philippe nodded in advance at his proposed
move. The King had a keen sense of his own interests:

if he had resolved to set the prisoner free, why should
he forgo the political benefit of his magnanimity? The
simple plot, as it did succeed, makes good comedy. At
any moment it might have taken a tragic turn: if caught,
the prince was determined not to survive.

The fortress was undergoing repairs; the prince himself had some alterations made at his own expense. Workmen from the outside moved to and fro under a scrutiny
that was to prove conveniently lax. Thélin, the prince's
valet, had procured a workman's outfit: rough shirt,
blouse, apron, blue trousers, thick-soled wooden shoes to
raise his height. The prince shaved his heavy mustache,
rouged his sallow cheeks, put on a long-haired black
wig. Then, a clay pipe in his mouth, a long shelf on his
shoulder, he sallied forth into freedom.

No one in the yard paid any attention to him. At the
gate the sergeant on duty raised his eyes from a letter he
was reading and nodded. The prince dropped his pipe
and, with a gesture of annoyance, picked up the pieces.
Just as he was leaving, he came across two workmen;
they glanced at him and vaguely thought he was one of
them: Bertrand (or Bertron, or Berthoud).

He was out of the citadel, but he was a long way
from the frontier. Had the countryside been alerted,
his chances would have been slim. Luck was with him:
Major Demarle, suffering from rheumatism, did not
make his morning inspection. To delay discovery, Dr.
Conneau used farcical but effective means. He gave out
that the prince was sick and had been dosed with castor
oil; and the ingenious doctor concocted convincing results with coffee, sops of bread, and nitric acid. Demarle
came around twice, and did not insist. After dinner, however, before writing his daily report, he had to see his

prisoner in person. Considerate to the last, he did not want to break the patient's uneasy slumber, and waited in the study. Then, thinking he heard the prince move, he entered the inner room. "Why, he is not breathing!" he cried. In sudden panic, he walked to the bed and shook the body. It was a dummy with a bandanna handkerchief round its head. "When did he escape?" he asked Conneau. "This morning, about seven." "I am disgraced!" said the major. With marvelous efficiency, he had the alarm sounded, the drawbridge raised, the gates bolted. The stable was safely locked, and the horse was far away.

In the meantime Thélin had met the prince with a carriage. Before reaching Saint-Quentin the fugitive shed his disguise. From Saint-Quentin a postchaise took the two men to Valenciennes. They arrived at two; the train for Brussels was due at four. At the station they were asked for their papers. Those of Thélin were in order; the prince's passed muster. A railway man, who had been a guard at Ham, recognized Thélin and asked him about his master. But their luck held. They boarded the train; there was no difficulty at the frontier. From Brussels they hurried to Ostend and thence to London.

Without delay, Louis-Napoleon made efforts to join his father. To no avail: the French government worked against him, and the Grand Duke of Tuscany refused his consent. King Louis died on July 26, 1846. He left his not inconsiderable fortune to his son.

The prince, now thirty-eight, was more than ever an exile, more than ever a pretender. How did he stand? He had matured. For the historians, his books *On Napoleonic Ideas* and *On the Extinction of Pauperism* were assets that balanced the blank failure of Strasbourg, the

ridiculous fiasco of Boulogne. Contemporaries, from
1846 to 1848, thought otherwise; or rather they did
not think at all: Louis-Napoleon was the Forgotten
Man.

Louis-Philippe had allowed King Jerome and his son,
Prince Napoleon, to return to France; he was considering granting them a pension. Politically—and finan-
cially—he could well afford it. This, to his mind, was
the epitaph of Bonapartism: there was not a spark of
life left in the cause, and the Emperor's family was but a
harmless historical monument. At the end of 1847 the
police reported on the activities of Legitimists and republicans; Bonapartism was not mentioned.

Never had Louis-Napoleon's goal seemed more unat-
tainable. It would take two revolutions, one five months
after the other, to give him his chance at last. But, we
must repeat, it would take also his obstinate faith and
his uncanny capacity for catching every political wind.

CHAPTER THREE

THE PRESIDENT
1848–1852

THE GERMANS called 1848 "the mad and holy year"; it was a time of apocalyptic hopes and fears. Anything might happen; everything did happen; everything failed, leaving the world sadder and not appreciably wiser. 1848 saw the last fireworks of expiring romanticism and the drab gray dawn of realism. This year of upheaval changed the destiny of Louis-Napoleon. So far he might be described as a minor character obstinately attempting to force his way to the center of the stage, and shoved back with scant courtesy. In 1848, given his cue, he strode boldly to the footlights. Without metaphors: in January he was an obscure pretender without a party; in December he was President of the French Republic by an overwhelming vote.

We must admit once again that mere biography can never grasp the whole truth. There are two extreme conceptions of history, the anecdotic and the philosophical, and we are condemned to hover between the two. The first will see only men of flesh and blood and the actual events in which they played a part. The second attempts to trace those immense trends which no individual can hope to start or deflect. The difference is mostly one of chronological scale. From day to day, from year to year, perhaps even from decade to decade, the biographical approach is right: personalities and incidents are the undeniable realities. In the perspective of cen-

turies, they fade and even vanish. If they survive at all,
it is as legends or symbols.

Because we are indulging for a moment in reflections
of a general nature, we must note that there may be a
discrepancy between events of dramatic significance and
their apparent causes. It is possible for great decisions to
go by default: in the lull before a revolution or a war,
we frequently find not grim unanimous determination,
but only passive, anxious bewilderment. Given time,
the people may come to believe, retrospectively, that
they have firmly *willed* their destiny. Given more time,
they may discover that this was a delusion. What we
call history unrolls itself on three planes. There is the
drama in which the actors, in full limelight, strut on the
stage and mouth their lines. In the background, there is
the atmosphere, the *Zeitgeist* as our fathers loved to call
it, the collective state of mind, which even in ages of
unity and faith is a welter rather than a philosophy, and
which is likely to change with disconcerting suddenness.
Then there are those obscure powers, spiritual and physical, which work in vast cycles, and sweep emperors with
their empires away, as floating debris is carried by a
swift-running flood.

As 1848 dawned, there seemed to be nothing radically wrong about the eighteen-year-old regime of Louis-
Philippe. A few annoying scandals in high circles, but
the royal family was above reproach, Marshal Soult's
looting days had long been over, and Guizot, the great
man of the reign, was a fine example of the Huguenot
conscience. There had been economic strains, poor crops,
a sharp recession in 1846-7, with the dull resentment
that such conditions inevitably create. But the constitu-

tion could not be blamed for these minor ills, and on the whole the country, in a cautious, unspectacular fashion, had been prospering under the July monarchy. No wars, and after 1840 no rumors of war. For those who found "peace in our time" unpalatable, there was the consolation of the Napoleonic Legend. For those eager to play soldiers, there were the colorful campaigns in Algeria. Only yesterday, one of the King's sons, d'Aumale, had captured the Smalah, or family and treasure, of the Emir Abd-el-Kader, and the Arab chieftain, defeated by Bugeaud, had surrendered to Lamoricière. A new France was opening up south of the Mediterranean. Already the stay-at-home bourgeois could assert with pride: "The Sahara is a French desert."

So the French throne seemed as solid as the other constitutional monarchies of northern Europe. The rot at the core was more insidious: disenchantment, listlessness, tedium. Even industry was timid. Thiers, the embodiment of bourgeois common sense, was sneering at the newfangled railways. Every prospect was dull: "France was bored." No remedy could be found for such an undefinable complaint because the men in power were so absolutely right in their own conceit. Guizot, the great doctrinaire and historian of civilization, was convinced that the middle class had been divinely appointed to follow the middle road, without which there was no salvation. He commanded a safe majority among the representatives of the wealthy: this was the country as defined by law, *le pays légal*, and he was satisfied. Only heavy taxpayers were shareholders in the great firm called France. When pressed for a change, Guizot shrugged his haughty shoulders: "If you want a vote, get rich!" This was not cynicism on his part: was not

wealth the test of solid worth, the natural reward of
enterprise and thrift?

Others, not radicals merely, republicans and socialists, but a moderate, loyal, "dynastic" opposition, were
not so easily pleased. They wanted a reform within the
Parliament: no more government officials in the Chamber, at the mercy of their superiors if they did not toe
the line. And they wanted an electoral reform: the
franchise should be extended to men of good education
and respectable standing, but of moderate means. In
those days political meetings were not allowed, but
public banquets were. Frugal feasts of cold veal and
salad were capped with heady oratory. And no man
could provide a richer brand than Lamartine: Lamartine the romantic poet and even more romantic historian;
Lamartine who, spurning the bourgeois Right and the
bourgeois Left, had declared that in the Chamber he
would sit "on the ceiling"; Lamartine, who claimed to
stand for "the constituency of the ideal." He threatened
the narrow materialists in power with "the revolution of
the public conscience, the revolution of contempt."

A banquet had been scheduled in Paris for February
22, 1848. The moderate opposition was of two minds:
there were elements in the capital that could easily turn a
legal demonstration into a riot. The government adopted
a "middle-of-the-road" attitude in the literal sense of that
absurd expression: it did not know which way it was
going. The banquet was forbidden, reluctantly authorized, and forbidden again, but with the proviso that the
matter would be taken before the courts. In fact, the conflict was no longer a tussle between two parliamentary
groups: it had become a battle between the people, un-

enfranchised and conscious of its natural rights, and the King, determined not to be bullied into submission.

In those tense hours, with mobs and patrols alternately sweeping the streets, peace was at the mercy of an incident. An isolated shot was fired; the soldiers, believing themselves attacked, responded with a volley. There was a number of dead; their corpses were carried through the city in tumbrils, rousing the masses to fury: "They are massacring the people!"

Louis-Philippe, aware at last of the peril, yielded, grudgingly, by inches, and always a minute too late. He sacrificed Guizot and called in Molé, his personal favorite—a futile move. Then Thiers, who had led the progressives; Odilon Barrot, head of the loyal opposition; Marshal Bugeaud, Duke of Isly, glorious and popular with his Algerian victories. But the flood kept rising beyond Molé, Thiers, Barrot, and Bugeaud.

In those days a few overturned buses, a few paving stones thrown into a heap, sufficed to barricade the narrow twisting lanes of the old city and turn whole districts into formidable fortresses. Cavalry and artillery could not be used effectively, and the insurgents, firing from the windows, had a definite advantage. The "king by the grace of the barricades" hesitated when barricades arose against him. His last hope was in the National Guard, composed of those bourgeois who had been the mainstay of his regime. He mounted his horse and passed the Guard in review. Instead of shouting: "Long live the King!" they cried: "Hurrah for the Reform!" The moral basis of the July monarchy had collapsed.

Louis-Philippe understood it all too well. It would have been possible, as Bugeaud advised, to withdraw from Paris, appeal to the country, and reconquer the capital. This is what Louis XVI had planned to do in the tragic flight that ended at Varennes; and it is what Thiers actually did in 1871 against the Commune. Louis-Philippe lacked neither physical courage nor determination. But he was in all sincerity a man of peace. He knew how slender his claims had been, and he did not want to start a civil war to maintain them. So he fled, rather hastily, without the sullen deliberation that had given the retreat of Charles X a character of somber majesty. As "Mr. Smith" he found refuge in England.

His sons, Joinville the Sailor Prince, and d'Aumale, so popular with the army, understood the lesson and offered no resistance. Had his eldest son, the Duke of Orléans, been alive, the revolution might have been averted; for the prince had been known to be liberal as well as capable. But he had died in an accident six years before. The heir, the Count of Paris, was a child of ten; the regent would have been his mother, a German princess. Their claims were disregarded as those of Chambord had been in 1830: fate is oddly fond of poetic justice.

The moderate reformers like Thiers and Barrot were in consternation. Their campaign for cautious progress had let loose a revolution. The shock troops were the radical elements in Paris: members of the secret societies, students more enthusiastic than responsible, workingmen who had not forgotten 1793, and the inevitable mob. This was 1830 over again; but this time the radicals were determined not to be tricked out of their victory. No more *Ersatz*-Republic, even if there had been a venerable Lafayette to give it his blessing. So they proclaimed at once a Democratic and Social Republic;

they had "the right to a job" affirmed as one of its essential principles; National Workshops were created; and Louis Blanc was soon to head a commission for the study of social problems. In three days (February 24–6) France jumped more than one hundred years ahead into uncharted regions: for the Fourth Republic is far more conservative than was the Second.

The miracle is that this sudden transformation was accepted at first without demur, and even with a certain degree of confidence and hope. The profit motive may be sensible, but it is not inspiring: few, even among the bourgeois, shed tears over the defunct July monarchy. The dull were accustomed to follow the fashions from Paris; the selfish were stunned, and held their peace. The opposition parties under Louis-Philippe, the Legitimists, the Republicans, the Socialists, as well as the inchoate Napoleonic sentiment, had different ideals: but they had this in common: that they stood for a faith, not for selfish gain. So there was a brief moment of communion among all men of good will. The clergy blessed the trees of liberty that were solemnly planted in every village square, and which, prophetically, refused to take root. France at that hour was indeed "the constituency of the ideal," and Lamartine became, as it were by natural right, the head of the provisional government.

We are not forgetting Louis-Napoleon in his London exile, for the events just related determined his course and permitted his rise. I have mentioned that Bonapartism and Orléanism had the same goal: to bring into harmony, as the Bourbons had been unable to do, the monarchy and the Revolution. But the methods were different. Orléanism stood for the golden mean—with

accent on the mean; Bonapartism had a sense of *grandeur*, which at its worst is the grandiose, and at its best
is greatness. It seems as though Louis-Napoleon had
constantly before his eyes the warning: "Above all, not
to be a Louis-Philippe." When he did become a Louis-
Philippe, in January 1870, the end was near.

Louis-Napoleon hastened from London to Paris while
Louis-Philippe was still on French soil. He came, he
said, as a free French citizen rallying to the flag of his
liberated country. The government, at that time, took
him neither tragically nor even seriously. But it hinted
that it had more pressing problems on hand than the
legal status of the Bonapartes, and that he would serve
France best by quietly returning to London. This he
did, with a clever letter in which he advertised his name
without revealing his full ambition. He felt it wiser to
wait until the smoke of battle had cleared, or until confusion had grown worse confounded.

There was in Lamartine a remarkable blend of generous idealism and cool-headed moderation. It was
thanks to him that the incredibly unstable combination of
February lasted until June; and thanks to him especially
that the general elections held on April 23 were a victory
for liberal, well-meaning republicans. They won 500
seats, and the extreme Left only 100. The Orléanists
had 200 deputies; the Legitimists 100. A Murat and a
Bonaparte were elected, but as republicans. The prince
himself had not been a candidate.

But uneasy makeshifts veiled by lofty oratory could
not indefinitely defer the crucial test. It was the radical
elements in Paris that had made the Revolution and created the Republic in their own image; but the bourgeoisie
in the cities, and the rural masses, after a moment of

stunned acquiescence, reasserted their essential conservatism. The Parisian leaders felt that their Republic was
slipping away from them. They tried to reaffirm the
sacred rights of the mob, which they equated with the
people's will. Radical demonstrations on March 17 and
April 16 miscarried, leaving the government weaker and
France more perturbed.

Had Louis-Napoleon been in the capital in those
days, there is little doubt that he would have sided with
the forces of order. Bonapartism as he conceived it was
to combine bold progressivism with strict discipline:
Napoleon III has been defined as "a cop with a dream."
On April 10, in London, when the conservative classes
dreaded a monster demonstration of the Chartists, Louis-
Napoleon took on the badge of a special constable and
actually stood on duty. It was a great good fortune for
him to be absent from Paris in those hours of confusion:
he was not committed either to revolution or to repression.

His luck held out: but for the fumbling of the provisional government, he might have been in Paris during
the tragic days of June. By-elections had been held on
June 4, and he had been elected by four constituencies;
but the government threatened to have him arrested if he
set foot in France; and although the Assembly voted to
admit him as a member, he preferred, in the interests of
peace, to tender his resignation. That was on June 15:
eight days later, Paris was aflame.

We have seen that on February 26, National Workshops had been created. The name was borrowed from
Louis Blanc; and the new institution was supposed to
implement the "right to a job," which had just been proclaimed. But the organization of the Workshops was

entrusted to a man who was a rabid antisocialist. A bold
program of public works could have made them effective; instead they were considered merely as emergency
relief and given nothing to do. Paris has always been a
great center of the luxury trades, which are the first to
suffer in a crisis. So the hordes of the unemployed were
mounting; they were sent to dig out the Champ-de-Mars
and then to fill it up again. Too old to find much pleasure in sand piles, the men downed their tools, lit their
pipes, and talked politics. So, while the financial burden
was becoming unbearable, a veritable army of subversion
was being assembled at the gate of Paris.

The government did not muster courage enough to
make the National Workshops a reality, but it found
courage enough to suppress them with a clumsiness and
a brutality that appeared intentional. For republican
Paris, this was the test: if the "right to a job" was to go,
the revolution of February had been fought and won in
vain. So the working quarters rose again. The insurrection was far more formidable than the impromptu riots
against Louis-Philippe. But this time the bourgeoisie,
forewarned, did not mean to capitulate. Lamartine's eloquence could not cope with such a crisis. His government was swept away, and a soldier hardened through
Algerian campaigns, General Godefroy Cavaignac, was
entrusted with dictatorial powers.

The fight was the most savage Paris had ever witnessed. Monseigneur Affre, archbishop of Paris, was
killed as he was attempting to utter a message of peace.
After three days of implacable struggle Cavaignac's victory was complete. He had "saved Society," but he had
killed the "Social and Democratic Republic" of February, and with it the liberal Republic of Lamartine. The

repression was pitiless: Cavaignac, an austere, high-minded republican, remained branded as "the Butcher of June."

On September 16, in new complementary elections, Louis-Napoleon was returned by five districts. This time there was no question of keeping him out. On the 24th he arrived in Paris, and again chose rooms within sight of the Vendôme Column. On the 26th he quietly took his seat in the National Constituent Assembly, an oddly unimpressive presence.

On October 9 a decisive debate took place on the method of electing the president. Many members were in favor of having him chosen by the Assembly: this would have resulted in the victory of General Cavaignac, who had been confirmed as Chief of the Executive Power. In an impassioned speech Lamartine favored direct election by the whole people. He may have thought that his own popularity, immense in February, had been veiled but not destroyed by the tragedy of June. But there is no reason to believe that he was not disinterested and sincere. There was a mystic side to his democratic faith. He accepted in earnest the dictum: *Vox populi vox Dei*. We should remember also that the political prestige of the American Republic ran high. Tocqueville, the author of *Democracy in America*, was a prominent member in the constitutional commission. Even Thiers had said: "In 1830 we crossed the Channel [i.e., we borrowed English precedents]; in 1848 we must be ready to cross the Atlantic."

Republicans who had watched with misgivings the rightist trend after the days of June wanted to bar from the presidency members of the families that had ruled over France. Representative Thouret offered an amend-

ment to that effect. Louis-Napoleon knew that such a
measure was directed chiefly against him: no Legitimist
and no Orléanist prince at that time appeared as a likely
candidate. He rose, went to the rostrum, spoke a few
words in his strange German-Swiss accent, closed
abruptly, and slouched back to his seat. Thouret, with
contemptuous irony, withdrew his amendment: in an assembly that reveled in oratory, a tongue-tied pretender
could hardly be considered a danger. This awkward
performance served Louis-Napoleon so well that he has
been accused of playing a part. It would have been a
dangerous game. The plain fact is that the prince, who
had a sonorous voice, a command of stately French, and
even, when conscious of his power, an impressive countenance, was a poor improviser. In this atmosphere which
was uncongenial and even hostile, he was quite naturally
at his worst.

On November 4 the constitution was carried. On the
25th, as a broad hint to the nation, the Assembly voted
that "General Cavaignac had deserved well of his father-
land." On December 10 the election was held; on the
20th the results were officially proclaimed. Louis-
Napoleon had received more than 5,300,000 votes;
Cavaignac, 1,400,000; Ledru-Rollin, the radical, 370,-
000; Raspail, the Socialist, 36,000; and Lamartine,
harmonious Lamartine, once the idol of the nation,
17,000. The prince took his constitutional oath; and—
this time in well-chosen words and with an assured voice
—made a brief appeal for concord. Cavaignac resigned
his power. He was perhaps too earnest to be a good
loser: he refused to shake hands with his successor.

The election on December 10, one of the decisive
events in modern French history, was difficult to inter-

pret at the time, and the difficulty has increased with the years. The verdict was emphatic, its sincerity indubitable. There could be no suspicion of force or fraud, and what official pressure was brought to bear worked in favor of the incumbent, General Cavaignac. Propaganda, at times of a rather blatant type, there certainly was. Persigny, who managed the campaign, must have reveled in the portraits, songs, broadsheets, in the clay pipes, jars, and knives bearing the candidate's effigy, with which he flooded the country. But *flooded* is an exaggeration: Louis-Napoleon's resources at that time were not un-limited, and his credit was none too good. And there was no lack of propaganda on the Cavaignac side.

Two obvious explanations should be, not lightly dis-missed, but examined with critical care. The first is that the election of a Napoleon, sight unseen, was simply the triumph of the Legend. It can hardly be denied that without the prestige of his name the prince would have had no chance. But we must not forget that the high-water mark of the Legend was in 1840, and that it had not saved the Emperor's nephew from ignominious fail-ure. Least of all was there in 1848 any popular clamor for martial glory. At that time it was the radicals who were urging a democratic crusade on behalf of Poland and Italy, and France shuddered at the prospect.

The second explanation is that the triumph of Louis-Napoleon was engineered by the Right, particularly by Thiers, a liberal frightened out of his wits by the threat of a social revolution. The monarchical Committee of the rue de Poitiers, not daring to put up a candidate of its own, endorsed the prince as the lesser of two evils: Cavaignac, a convinced republican, would have con-solidated the Republic. Those astute politicians knew, or thought they knew, that the pretender was a dolt. In the presidential chair he would be their puppet; when the time came to get rid of him, he could be removed as easily as he had been arrested at Strasbourg and at Boulogne. Some German conservatives, including a number of wealthy Jews, played the same Machiavellian game with Adolf Hitler.

If such was the hope of Thiers and his friends, they fooled themselves with remarkable thoroughness. I must speak with caution, for the record is not clear. My own interpretation is that Louis-Napoleon would have won without the support of the organized monarchists. They felt the wave, at the same time popular and conservative, that suddenly surged in his favor. They attempted to ride that wave. If that interpretation be valid, their move was shrewd. They did manage to create a confusion; they could without absurdity claim that the President was their man. To use current slang again, they "muscled in"; and this helped them in the general elections of March 13, 1849.

We pardonably desire clear-cut answers to definite questions, but history refuses to oblige. The first great cause of Louis-Napoleon's success was negative: every other party had been engulfed in failure. The Restoration had never been popular, even in its wan heyday; by 1848 Legitimism was the creed of a few respectable fossils, country squires, and unworldly priests. Orléanism had crashed only ten months before. The idealistic republic of Lamartine had proved a flimsy hope. The Reds had been crushed in June. Louis-Napoleon alone, miraculously kept out of harm's way, was untried and therefore unsullied. In the political vacuum he suddenly loomed enormous.

But there was a more positive cause, for which he deserves personal credit. Thanks to his publications, his name was a program, and that program had something to offer to all the classes. To the lesser bourgeoisie and the peasant proprietors, who between them formed the solid masses of the country, Bonapartism meant a strong police state that would maintain material order, repress any "share-the-wealth" nonsense (*les partageux*) and exorcise "the Red Specter." But the same conservative classes dreaded a return to the ancient regime: Napoleon I, in their eyes, had been a sovereign of democratic origins, attached to "the immortal principles of 1789." Even some of the Reds distrusted the new Cæsar less than they hated Cavaignac, "the Butcher of June." Was not Louis-Napoleon a disciple of Louis Blanc, and had he not written *On the Extinction of Pauperism*? In the confusion and frustration of the hour he alone stood clearly for the motto of the Positivist Auguste Comte, which Brazil was to adopt as its national device: *Order and Progress*. If Louis-Napoleon was thus all things to all men, it was not out of unscrupulous eclecticism: "Tell me what you want, and I'll promise it to you." It was because, for a moment at least, his inner complexities had reached a precarious balance, and that they matched exactly the complexities of the national mind. In the most literal sense, he was the Man of the Hour.

Louis-Napoleon began his term of office with unimpeachable correctness. No trumpets of jubilee announced a new era or even a new deal. To be sure, he was no mere bourgeois executive: he was styled Prince-President, wore the uniform of a general in the National Guard, and introduced an unobtrusive but semi-regal

etiquette in his residence, the Élysée. He picked out as
Premier an unobjectionable middle-road parliamentarian,
Odilon Barrot, who had led the "loyal opposition" under
Louis-Philippe. On January 29, the new President
showed quiet efficiency in quelling incipient disorder.

The Roman expedition is often cited as proof of a
bargain between Louis-Napoleon as a candidate and the
reactionary group known as the Groupe de la rue de
Poitiers. The facts are more complex. The Roman problem had already worried the Cavaignac administration.
Rome had rebelled against the absolutism of the Pope,
Pius IX, who, frightened by the murder of his minister
Rossi, had fled to Gaeta on November 25, 1848. On
February 9, 1849 a Roman Republic had been proclaimed. On March 30 the French Assembly (still the
old Constituent, which, its task long accomplished, was
tenaciously clinging to life) had authorized sending an
observation corps to Civita Vecchia to forestall Austrian
intervention, and, as the Premier, Odilon Barrot, put it,
"for the protection of liberal institutions." Louis-Philippe
had set a precedent when, for the same purpose, he had
sent troops to occupy Ancona.

The Constituent Assembly, with its bewildered and
discouraged Lamartinian majority, dissolved at last. In
the elections to the Legislative Assembly (May 13), the
moderate Republicans shrank from 500 to 80; the extreme Left increased from 100 to 180. The Party of
Order, in aggressive mood after the events of the previous
year, won a sweeping victory, with 460 seats. There
was no presidential party: it was the aim of Louis-
Napoleon to stand above the strife as the representative
of national interests. A few personal friends were known

as the group of the Élysée. Oddly enough, Victor Hugo was mentioned among them.

Still a correct executive, the President did not attempt to govern against the overwhelming majority of the Chamber. The Roman expedition, through a series of misunderstandings rather than through a decisive shift in policy, changed its character: it was now frankly aimed at the destruction of Mazzini's Republic, and at the restoration of the Pope's temporal power. Even then, in a letter which was made public, Louis-Napoleon expressed the hope that the pontiff would return as a liberal sovereign. An abortive revolution in Paris on June 13 frightened the conservatives into repressive measures: the Reds should be put down in France as they had been in Rome. This reactionary turn did not originate with the President, but neither did he oppose it. He was not the wholehearted ally of the conservatives; he seemed rather to be their prisoner.

Odilon Barrot no longer represented a workable compromise between President and Assembly. He was dismissed on October 31, 1849. But instead of forming a rightist cabinet, Louis-Napoleon appointed a lackluster administration of practical men: d'Hautpoul, Achille Fould, Eugène Rouher. This marked without bluster the change from a parliamentary to a presidential government. The executive and the legislative were now going each its own way; and it might take them very far apart.

The French constitution of 1848 had not provided for such a contingency. Neither, for that matter, has the American. The result of this ambiguity is that America has in fact two unwritten constitutions: under a strong popular executive—a Jackson, a Lincoln, a Theodore

Roosevelt, a Wilson, a Franklin Roosevelt—the predominance of the executive is manifest. If opinion is
evenly divided, or if the executive is not a commanding personality, the regime becomes almost pure parlia-
mentarism. The American Constitution has stood the
strain; the French did not. The difference is not owing
to some purely technical flaw or to the political temper
of the two peoples. America never was seriously threatened either by a revolution of the Right or by a revolution of the Left: the France of 1850 was imperiled
by both.

Faithful to his principle, and to the origin of his
power, the President took the matter to the people as
the supreme arbiter. He remained strictly within the
framework of the constitution; but he seized every opportunity—public works, national festivals, military reviews—to travel in every part of the country, to be seen
and to be heard. "The man who has been elected by six
million voters," he said (rather generously rounding the
figure), "carries out the will of the citizens, and does not
betray them." Some thought that this enigmatic sentence
was a promise that there would be no *coup d'état*. It
meant, more obviously, that if the President, in harmony with the great majority of the people, was compelled to act against the Assembly, and even against the
letter of the constitution, he would feel justified.

Everywhere, even in the cities known for their leftist
sympathies, such as Lyon and Strasbourg, the President
was received with an enthusiasm that no official claque
could have produced. France was weary of political
squabbles, and there was a mounting dread of an upheaval in 1852. It was palpable that neither the Right
nor the Left had any love or respect for the ailing Re-

public. The conservatives wanted to make their present advantage permanent through a monarchical restoration. They were aware that this would mean bloodshed, for the great cities were ardently republican. But they affirmed their determination "to reach the Promised Land even though they had to cross the Red Sea." The radicals felt that the crest of the reactionary wave was over; they would have had a good chance of winning at the polls in 1852 if the conditions were equitable. But the conservative majority had rigged up an electoral law that disfranchised nearly three million voters, one third of the electorate, most of them workingmen and republicans. So the Left, convinced that *their* republic had been stolen from them, swore that they would reconquer it, if need be through another revolution.

The two major parties were thus openly preparing civil war. In that situation the President was the only symbol of unity and the only guarantee of peace. His powers were to expire in 1852, and he could not be re-elected. An amendment to the constitution on this point was proposed, and seventy-nine departmental councils endorsed it, only six voicing opposition. In the Assembly the more reasonable conservatives, realizing the urgency of the situation, were ready to vote for it. In the final ballot, there were 446 ayes to 278 noes; but in this case a three-fourths majority was required (534 to 181), and the motion was lost. So the system could neither work nor be mended; and there was no legal means of brushing it out of the way.

England has not had a violent change of government since the end of the seventeenth century; America none since the end of the eighteenth. But in France, within the memory of living men, seven governments had met a violent death: in 1792, 1799, 1814, twice in 1815, in 1830, and only three years before, in 1848. The imminence of a sudden stroke was an open secret: the date and the method remained uncertain.

The Assembly, seeing its defenses crumble, stood resentful but helpless. The Right had counted on General Changarnier, whom Louis-Napoleon had placed in command both of the National Guard and of the regular troops in Paris. Changarnier was a bluff, jovial soldier with a healthy sense of his popularity and importance. He thought of himself as indispensable, but he could not quite make up his mind to whom. He had scant respect for the Prince-President, whom he called— the phrase was apt—"a melancholy parrot." He boasted that if the need were to arise, he could imprison Louis-Napoleon in the fortress of Vincennes. Suddenly, on January 3, 1851, the President dismissed him. He was within his constitutional rights, and Changarnier did not dare to challenge the decision. The most prominent members of the conservative party waited on the President, urging him to change his mind. He was, as Hortense had described him in his childhood, gently obstinate. And Thiers gloomily prophesied: "The Empire is made!"

One last open move, and a very shrewd one. On November 4, 1851 the President asked the Assembly to repeal the obnoxious electoral law of May 31, 1850, which had deprived three million citizens of their vote. The Assembly fell into the trap and rejected his proposal. So he could pose as the champion of universal (manhood) suffrage, one of the essential conquests of 1848.

Meanwhile, Louis-Napoleon was quietly maturing his plans. This time he did not indulge in a wild gamble. First of all, he needed money. Always a lavish spender, he had long ago dissipated Hortense's heritage, a loan from the eccentric Duke of Brunswick, and the moderate fortune of King Louis. The Assembly had refused to increase his presidential stipend. But his staunch supporter Achille Fould was wealthy. The Spanish Ambassador, Marshal Narváez, Duke of Valencia, was willing to take a risk. And Miss Howard still believed in him: she had some hope of becoming, if not an Empress Theodora, at any rate a modern Pompadour.

With money in his purse, Louis-Napoleon was organizing his task force. He alone was the master mind: the members of the team were his chosen instruments. Leroy de Saint-Arnaud was picked out as a vigorous soldier without squeamishness. A campaign in Kabylia furnished a pretext for promoting him, and he was made Minister of War. The army of Paris was placed under Magnan. Maupas, credited with an iron fist, became prefect of police. The faithful Persigny, of course, was on hand. For the key position, the Ministry of the Interior, Louis-Napoleon picked out Count de Morny.

Morny was the son of Queen Hortense and Count de Flahaut, himself the natural son of Talleyrand. He was proud of his origin. On his coat of arms he had an eagle rising out of a bush of *hortensias* (hydrangea), with the device: *Tace sed memento* (Be silent, but remember). Until the Revolution of 1848 the half-brothers had never met. Louis-Napoleon was among the few who did not know the secret of Morny's birth. He was shocked at first, for his filial love had a touch of veneration (he went so far as to believe in the virtue of the Empress

Josephine). There was a marked physical resemblance between the two men. Both were adventurers who had to carve their way. But Louis-Napoleon had a faith, and Morny had none. In their association, interest and affection became curiously mingled. Morny alone could address Napoleon III in the unconventional form: "My dear Emperor."

After a brief career as an officer in Algeria, Morny had made his fortune in Paris under Louis-Philippe. His father, Flahaut, had an honored place in society; the young man became the personal friend of the Orléans princes; he remained an Orléanist at heart even when he became the second personage in the Second Empire. He played admirably, because sincerely, the part of the aristocrat who toys with finances, politics, and the arts, but remains superior to place, money, fame—and principles. He was a Count d'Orsay with a genius for business; a gambler at the same time reckless and cool; an epicure with a will of steel. Compared with him, Persigny was crude and honest.

The Élysée, December 1, 1851. The regular Monday evening reception. The President calls aside Colonel Vieyra, of the National Guard: "Can you hear a secret and not give a twitch?" "I can." "Well, it is for tonight." The colonel bowed: in the night, every drum in the Guard was stove in so that the alarm could not be sounded: a small instance of conspiratorial thoroughness. At ten thirty, six men gathered in the President's study: the prince himself; Mocquard, his confidential secretary; the inevitable Persigny; Morny, Maupas, Saint-Arnaud. The prince opened a bundle of papers marked "Rubicon." The last directions were given. The proclamations were sent to the National Printing Shop. Soldiers were to keep close watch over the workmen so as to prevent any leak. "We are risking our skins," Morny remarked airily. "Mine is old, and not worth much," Mocquard replied. And the prince, as if to rebuke their levity, concluded: "Have no fear: I am wearing my mother's ring, with the word *Hope*." Eleven, and the Élysée was asleep.

Between five and six o'clock Paris was placarded with white posters: white in France is reserved for official documents. There was a Presidential Decree, a Proclamation to the Army, an Appeal to the People. By the decree, the Assembly was dissolved and—a master stroke—universal suffrage restored. The acts of the President would be submitted to the people as a whole. An outline of the proposed constitution was given: it was closely modeled on that of the Consulate. Before dawn some seventy political leaders were arrested, Thiers among them, and the generals whose prestige and independence might have endangered the success of the move: Cavaignac, Bedeau, Changarnier, Lamoricière. Colonel Espinasse occupied the Palais-Bourbon, seat of the Assembly. Three notes on the bugle were sounded, announcing that everything had proceeded without a hitch.

In the dismal light of a winter morning, early risers were gazing at the white posters. There was no indignation, but some shrugs: "It had to come!" some smiles: "Well played!" At ten, a cavalcade of officers sallied forth from the Élysée: old King Jerome, Magnan, Saint-Arnaud, and their staff. At the head, alone, unprotected, rode the President. There was no tumultuous applause, but there was no ominous silence either. Paris admired the daring and the skill of the stroke, and was not un-friendly; but it remained reserved.

Of legal resistance there was practically none. Du-pin, chairman of the Assembly, refused to act. The ar-rested deputies were not harshly treated, and they were soon released. The masses refused to rise: the Assembly stood for confused, half-hearted reaction, and had no friends. Perfunctory barricades arose, and were aban-doned at first sight of the troops. Victor Hugo and a few radicals went from one district hall to another, pass-ing resolutions, pasting soul-stirring and pitiful little handbills on the walls. They had to recognize with anger and shame that Paris was indifferent: it simply refused to recognize the Assembly as the sole rampart of democracy. So the 2nd of December could be con-sidered as a success for the President, although there was no surge of enthusiasm.

The 3rd was a sullen, indecisive day. The President was strongly advised not to venture again in the streets: a stray bullet, and the whole elaborate scheme would collapse. A rumor spread that General Neumayer, with an army loyal to the Assembly, was marching on Paris. The activities of Hugo and his friends, although they could not nerve the people to heroic resistance, had at any rate created misgivings. A few barricades went up again. But the masses remained indifferent. Dr. Baudin, a representative, was attempting to rouse the onlookers. He was answered with a shrug and a jeer: "Get our-selves killed so that you will draw your twenty-five francs a day? Guess again!" "Citizens," Baudin replied, "I'll show you how one dies for twenty-five francs." He mounted the barricades and was shot dead. Like most historical words, these may be apocryphal. The episode is part of French folklore: the one thing it proves is that the workers declined to fight.

Strangely, the stray barricades were built without serious interference on the part of police or troop: Maupas and Magnan had withdrawn their men from the areas of disturbance. This looked like hesitancy, and the republicans took heart. It was no retreat, however, on the part of the President's forces, but a strategic move. Among the chief agents of the *Coup d'État*, some were not satisfied with their half-success: they wanted a showdown and a clear-cut victory. On the 4th the troops came back in force and reduced the barricades with little difficulty. Perhaps Magnan and Maupas, small men without scruples, were eager to magnify their share in the enterprise. In the dim background we feel the presence of Napoleon's chief lieutenant, Morny. He knew the democratic and even socialistic propensities of his brother, and the ambivalent character of his policy. "Society had to be saved," and the new government must give evidence that it could be tough.

The eloquent resistance of Victor Hugo, materially so futile, and the brutal display of force on December 4, changed the character of the *Coup d'État*. From a bold and generous appeal to the people, it was turned into a victory for "order," the existing order, the citadel of economic privilege, and into a disaster for the "subversives," the believers in the social and democratic Republic of February 1848.

This new aspect, not foreseen and not desired by Louis-Napoleon, was emphasized by two accidents. The troops were marching along the boulevards. A well-dressed crowd, women and children among them, watched them without hostility or fear. Again, as in February 1848, a shot was fired. Again the soldiers, made nervous by three days of tension and fatigue, fired back at random, without orders. Unit after unit, hear-ing the fusillade, caught the panic and fired in its turn. It took long minutes to restore discipline; when the brief spasm was over, the sidewalks were littered with wounded and dead.

The second accident—for genius is an accident, a *lusus naturæ*—is that Victor Hugo, who had morally led the fight, was to tell the story; and Hugo was the greatest poet of his time; at any rate, the most obviously great. He had worshipped Napoleon I; he had been the friend of his nephew, and a welcome guest at the Élysée. Now he could, with a clear conscience, strike a magnificent attitude of defiance. The results were *Na-poleon the Little, Chastisements, History of a Crime:* when the Empire fell, the indictment was ready in words of undying fire. Woe to the ruler who provokes a mod-ern Ezekiel.

Destiny played a crooked game with Napoleon III, who, for his part, was not the mirror of rectitude. No victory of his was ever unequivocal and final. He ex-pected the *Coup d'État* to be an apotheosis, and a few days later (December 20–1), an enormous popular vote, 7,440,000 to 646,000, was to ratify his action. But there was a moral flaw in this triumph. Louis-Napoleon sincerely believed himself to be the ruler of France "by the grace of God and the will of the peo-ple." A sardonic addition could not be silenced: "not to mention fraud and force, Morny and Saint-Arnaud."

CHAPTER FOUR

THE EMPEROR
1852–1870

IN 1800, when the text of the Consular Constitution was placarded on the walls of Paris, one citizen was nonplussed by its apparent complication. Another reassured him: "It is all very simple: there are only two words that matter, *Napoleon Bonaparte*." In this respect as in so many others, the constitution ratified on December 20–1, 1851 by an overwhelming plebiscite resembled its Consular model. Behind the elaborate legal phraseology, there was only one stark fact, Cæsarism. The constitution was not officially proclaimed until January 14, 1852. But already on New Year's Day the President had left the unassuming Élysée for the Tuileries, the ancient abode of French sovereigns. The stodgy days of bourgeois republicanism were over.

The constitution provided for a president elected for ten years by the people, and responsible only to the people. No cabinet in the parliamentary sense: the ministers were merely the president's secretaries. He was to be advised by an élite of technicians, the Council of State: an excellent institution with roots deep in the royal past, it had received its final form, not substantially altered to this day, under the Consulate. It was the Council of State that had elaborated, with Napoleon's active participation, the famous Civil Code, of which he was prouder than of any of his victories.

A Senate, composed of life members, was to bring together "the most illustrious personages in France."

76   NAPOLEON III

Its duties were mostly honorific: the Senate was to consider petitions from the people, and to act as the guardian of the "Fundamental Pact." The name had prestige,
the stipend was handsome, the work was light. A seat in
the Senate was a fit reward for those faithful followers
of the prince who preferred not to engage in more strenuous and responsible activities. The ideal Senator was
King Jerome.

Last and least came a Legislative Body elected by
manhood suffrage. Its initiative was strictly limited; its
debates were reported in barest outline. To discourage
the streams of eloquence which had been the glory and
the plague of the constitutional monarchy, each member was to speak, not from the rostrum, but from his
own seat.

There was a slight flutter among the President's closest followers when, on January 23, 1852, he confiscated
by decree certain properties of the Orléans family and
turned over the proceeds to social works. This was not
a tyrannical whim, and not a personal vendetta against
the fallen regime: Louis-Napoleon's act had some color
of justification. According to immemorial tradition, the
personal domains of a new king were merged with those
of the crown, for the crown and France were one. Louis-
Philippe, immensely wealthy in his own right as Duke
of Orléans, had failed to follow that precedent. Modern
kingship is a precarious business, and the new sovereign
was shrewd enough in 1830 to have some premonition
of 1848. So, before ascending the throne, he divested
himself of his property in favor of his children. His foresight proved only too accurate, and we can hardly blame
him for it. Louis-Napoleon, of a more reckless temper,
never appreciated that kind of cleverness. He was only

too willing to merge his estates—that is, his debts—with the national treasury. Above all, he wanted to prove that although the monarchists obstinately rallied to him, he was not their servant. It was, on a more humane level, his Duke of Enghien affair. Several of his ministers—Rouher, Magne, Fould—resigned; and even his second in command in the great adventure of the *Coup d'État*, his own brother, Morny. All of them eventually returned to the fold.

It was a sign of Louis-Napoleon's great personal popularity that their gesture did not weaken his hold on the country. The elections that took place a month later (February 29, 1852) were a landslide in his favor. Out of 261 members, 253 were docile, one might say automatic, in their loyalty. Posters of official white had indicated that they were the President's choice: the electorate, firmly guided by the prefects, had meekly followed their leader. Such unanimity invariably arouses suspicion. But even a leftist historian like Charles Seignobos admits that the elections gave a fair picture of the public mind, perhaps artfully but discreetly touched up. After all, "the Red Specter" was a reality in those days, and in our free America the Reds do not hold even a single seat. Of the dissenters, the three Legitimists and the three Republicans sat in helpless and taciturn reproof. Only one voice was heard in the muffled hall, that of the Catholic orator Montalembert, "a penitent Christian, an impenitent liberal." Frightened by the prospect of a social revolution, he had approved of the *Coup d'État;* but he was unwilling to accept its consequences. He could never forget that God had fashioned him to speak eloquently, and the Assembly he addressed was willfully and congenitally deaf. All through the Em-

pire, spurned by the Left as undemocratic, rejected by
his fellow Catholics as tainted with liberalism, he was to
waste his undeniable talent in ambiguous controversies.

In spite of Thiers's dire prophecy early in 1851:
"The Empire is made!" Louis-Napoleon seemed in no
hurry to change his title. For years he had quietly
prophesied: "When I am Emperor of the French . . ."
but it was still as President that he made a triumphal
tour of central and southern France. He had the reality
of power, but the name was not without significance.
For one thing, it would be a reparation due to his
uncle's memory: twice the Empire had been destroyed
by the victors. This *Diktat* rankled, just as after 1919
the guilt clause rankled in the German mind; France
would not feel herself free until the last traces of the
hated Vienna settlement had been effaced. A crown is
but a bauble; but to the earnest believer, a bauble may
be a revered symbol, and the imperial crown was the
sign of alliance between the Grace of God and the Will
of the People. What burned in Louis-Napoleon's
heart with religious intensity was also felt by the masses
in a looser, but still very real, way. Obviously they had
not elected and confirmed a Napoleon as head of the
State in order to have a mere president. Many were convinced that the Empire alone could bar the way to the
two flags France dreaded almost equally, the red and
the white.

So Louis-Napoleon was not surprised when everywhere he heard the crowds shout: "Long live the Emperor!" By the time he reached Bordeaux, he felt so
sure of his ground that, on October 9, in a notable
speech, he gave out the program of his future reign. To

modern ears, there is a Mussolinian ring about his promises of efficiency and prosperity. There were marshes to
be drained in both countries—a realistic plan with sym-
bolic overtones. The Extinction of Pauperism, the
moral and material welfare of the most numerous and
poorest classes—these were the implied promises. The
Empire was not to be merely "the field freely open to
all the profiteers." There was in the public mind one
great objection to a restored Empire: if it openly challenged the treaties of Vienna, would it not revive the
era of armed conflicts? Louis-Napoleon, with the same
sincerity as Woodrow Wilson and Franklin Roosevelt,
pledged his word that he would keep France out of
war: *"L'Empire, c'est la paix."*

The Senate, on a nod from the master, decided that
the people should be consulted about this amendment
to the Fundamental Pact. On November 21 a plebiscite approved the restoration of the Empire by 7,824,-
000 to 253,000. On December 1, at Saint-Cloud, the
President was officially notified of the result. His reign
began the next day, December 2. Thus were com-
memorated the first Napoleon's coronation (1804), his
most brilliant victory, Austerlitz (1805), and the *Coup
d'État* of 1851.

In his *Napoleonic Ideas* the prince had forecast a
head of the state with the title of Emperor, but elected
for ten years only. What the plebiscite had re-established
was the hereditary, the dynastic Empire. We cannot
help wondering what the place of the two Napoleons
would have been in history if the first had governed from
1799 to 1809, and the second from 1851 to 1861.

It was inevitable that the new sovereign should be
called Napoleon III: there actually had been a Na-

poleon II. He had been proclaimed on June 22, 1815,
according to a constitution ratified by a plebiscite. At
the origin of many monarchies—the Roman Empire itself, its interminable shadow, the Holy Roman Empire
of the German Nation, and even the French Capetian
line—we find the same willful confusion between he-
redity and popular choice. A dynasty remains legitimate—that is, representative—as long as it keeps true
to its original principle. Napoleon III believed himself
to be, not merely an heir, but a second Founder; by
making the Cæsarian democracy of Napoleon I explicit,
he had given it a new life. He considered that his claims
were based, not on his imperial blood alone, but on his
spontaneous and triumphal election on December 10,
1848. A new street in the center of Paris, symbolically
leading from the Stock Exchange to the Opéra, was
called *rue du Dix-Décembre*. It is now *rue du Quatre-
Septembre*, in commemoration of the day when the Empire fell.

A republic has one tremendous advantage: France
does not have to worry about the uncles and cousins of
President Coty. But in 1852, when she made Napoleon
an emperor, she saddled herself with the whole Bonaparte clan. It was a large and interesting connection,
with a full quota of black sheep; one of them, Pierre
Bonaparte, endangered the regime in 1870. Some were
of a decent neutral tint: an ornithologist, a Basque
scholar, a cardinal. The only one with any claim to
brilliancy was far from lovable. On the whole, they were
a doubtful asset to ruler and country. Napoleon III recognized this fact at least twice. His stormy cousin,
Prince Napoleon, the son of King Jerome, once taunted

him: "You have nothing in common with the great Emperor!" and he replied: "Alas! I have his family." And, proclaiming to the people his choice of an empress, he mentioned as a crowning grace: "And she has no relatives to be provided for."

There were at least two sons of Napoleon I alive in 1852. We have already come across Count Léon: he was paid a pension and kept at arm's length. The Viennese historian August Fournier mentioned three more: Count Walewski; a certain Devienne, who had vanished altogether; and John Gordon, who died in San Francisco in 1885. We have a photograph of this Gordon, dated 1871: his resemblance to his alleged father is indeed remarkable. But, as he was born five or six years after Napoleon's death, the resemblance must be purely coincidental. The Count of Chambord, posthumous son of the Duke of Berry, and last scion of the elder Bourbon line, was called "the Child of the Miracle"; the John Gordon miracle would have been of far greater magnitude.

Walewski, on the other hand, stands in the full light of history, and he stands surprisingly well. In 1809 Countess Walewska sacrificed herself, as she thought, in the interest of her country, Poland; Alexander Colonna Walewski was the child of that patriotic gesture. Napoleon played fast and loose with the hopes of the Poles, but he sincerely loved Marie; she was perhaps, apart from Josephine, the only woman he did love. In 1814 she took the boy on a visit to Elba; in 1815 mother and son bade Napoleon farewell after Waterloo.

Brought up as a Polish patriot, loyal to his country, and to the man whose name he bore, Walewski left Poland in order to avoid serving in the Russian army.

He returned at the time of the first great uprising
(1830–1). When it was crushed, he became a French
subject, served in Algeria, and, as the protégé of Thiers,
played a secondary but creditable part in diplomacy.
His countenance betrayed his origin, which he acknowledged in proud silence. His cousin Napoleon III made
him his special envoy to London, and his Minister of
Foreign Affairs. This was the highest point in his career:
in 1856, as French Plenipotentiary, he presided over
the Congress of Paris. His other functions and honors—
Senator, Minister of State, President of the Legislative
Body, Duke—were but wreaths commemorating that
one great moment.

So handsome, so successful, so dignified a personage
would inevitably be accused of conceit. We are rather
surprised, on the contrary, to find so much serious worth
under the impressive mask and the gilded uniform. He
had been more than a dabbler in literature, and his salon
was noted for intellectual and artistic distinction. Perhaps his faultless and aloof dignity was but a carapace
for the protection of his wounded pride. He was sensitive enough to realize the hollowness of his splendid position: even when he was Minister of Foreign Affairs,
he never was in the full confidence of Napoleon III. It
was whispered that the Emperor was far more intimate
with Countess Walewska, a handsome and vivacious
Florentine; "only," it was said in mock extenuation, "in
order to follow his uncle's example."

The imperial court was not in the least hampered by
"legitimist" prejudices: better be the natural son of a
strong and clever man than the legal offspring of a dul-
lard. Morny, grandson of Talleyrand, son of Flahaut
and Hortense, looked upon his origin as princely. We

have caught a glimpse of him as the chief instrument of Louis-Napoleon's *Coup d'État*. He sulked for a while when the President confiscated the Orléans domains, but he re-entered public life as a magnificent and most successful Ambassador to Russia; then he was, until his death, President of the Legislative Body. His political services were unobtrusive, but essential. In the brilliant but slightly erratic course of the regime, he was both a balance wheel and an ornament. His official residence, *le Petit Bourbon*, gave the tone to society more than the vast nondescript court at the Tuileries, or the Palais-Royal of King Jerome and Prince Napoleon.

It is fascinating to compare the two sons of Hortense: they had much in common, for good and for evil. But it was the error of Victor Hugo, Kinglake, Rochefort, to consider Napoleon as merely another, and perhaps a lesser, Morny. In essentials, they were poles asunder. Morny, for all his sophistication and *savoir-faire*, was obvious. Subtract from Napoleon's enigmatic personality the undeniable, the very large Morny element, and what remains is, not the key to the mystery, but the mystery itself.

Even physically there was a striking likeness between them. Both became bald early; but Morny's baldness was patent, almost d'Annunzio-like; Napoleon's was concealed with long locks artfully waved over his forehead. Both had prominent noses; but Napoleon's was exaggerated, and could be likened to a parrot's bill. Both had drooping lids and eyes that told no tales. But Morny's were wary, with a touch of superciliousness; Napoleon's gentle gravity was impenetrable. Morny was a little taller, longer-legged. He had none of that shuffling gait which Anatole France compared with the waddling

of a great sea-bird. Morny was seen at his best in a
drawing-room, with faultless evening dress; Napoleon,
in uniform, on horseback.

Both, if adventurers, were born aristocrats: their
manners were exquisite, Morny's with a dash of eighteenth-century impertinence, inherited from Talleyrand,
Napoleon's with the simplicity that becomes an acknowledged prince. They had to carve out for themselves,
through daring and cunning, a destiny commensurate
with their origin: bourgeois scruples had little weight
with them. Not cruel at heart, they could be ruthless.
In the hour of danger they kept a cool head. Fate had
made them gamblers: Morny in the crudest sense—the
card table, the races, the Stock Exchange—Napoleon
for higher stakes—a throne, the reconstruction of Europe, the shaping of a new society. Aristocrats though
they were, they yielded to the temptation of display, the
gambler's gloating over his gains: in a sense, they were
parvenus. Morny affected to give deeper thought to the
details of his luxury than to his official duties. He was
something of a connoisseur; his picture gallery was as
notable as his stable and his cuisine. Under the name of
Monsieur de Saint-Rémy, he wrote bright little farces,
one of which, *Monsieur Choufleury will Be at Home*,
kept its sparkle for a season. Napoleon's mind dwelt on
other things. In the decoration of life, he paid the bills,
uncritically. He had very little interest in art or literature;
much in archæology. He devoted his spare moments to
a monumental *Life of Cæsar*.

In St. Petersburg, Morny won as his bride a Princess
Troubetzkoy, of no great wealth, but of ancient lineage.
Unconventional, yet thoroughly conservative in her out-
look, she despised the motley court of the Tuileries. She

added to her husband's splendid establishment an elfin
note of fantasy, half exotic, half childlike. The Petit
Bourbon, with its priceless art treasures, with its famous
Chinese drawing-room, with its large cage of monkeys,
was too well appointed to be called bohemian, but it was
whimsical almost to the point of self-irony. Its atmosphere hovered between Louis Quinze refinement and
the hectic gaiety of an Offenbach operetta. Morny was
genuinely fond of his wife, but in a *grand seigneur*, Tal-
leyrand-like fashion. For—last point of resemblance—
both sons of Hortense played ardently, in advancing
years, the treacherous game of chance that the French
call *l'amour*. At fifty, Morny, a fast liver, wanted to live
even faster; he drugged himself in a haphazard and disastrous fashion. He died exhausted at fifty-four. At the
last moment the brothers were left alone. What thoughts
passed between them, what silent deathbed confessions,
not even a Proust or a Musil could validly surmise.

The Empire gave the duke, as he had become, a
funeral of princely magnificence; many felt the chill of
death passing over the regime. No one thought of Morny
as a great man, and least of all as a good man; but he
had been a pleasant associate, and had managed to play
down rancor. So he was universally regretted, at court, in
financial circles, in society. Even his wife mourned for
him: she cut her long tresses and had them buried in his
bier. But she did not weep for long: he had not been
thorough enough in the destruction of his private correspondence, and the bereaved duchess understood him
at last. Three years later, she was Duchess of Sesto. Of
his role in the evolution of the regime, I shall have a few
words to say later.

·   ·   ·

At the summit of the imperial family stood Napoleon's uncle, King Jerome, and his two children, Princess Mathilde and Prince Napoleon. King Jerome, the
youngest brother of the great Emperor, was the last link
with the first Empire. He was treated as a precious relic:
Governor of the Invalides, and thus guardian of his
brother's tomb; Marshal of France; President of the
Senate, with the Palais-Royal as his residence, and a
princely income. He had been, next to Canova's lovely
model, Pauline Borghese, the most amiable and the
least responsible of the Bonapartes. As König Hierony-
mus in the puppet Kingdom of Westphalia, he had left
the memory of a merry and particularly incompetent
monarch. In the Russian campaign he had proved an in-
efficient corps commander, and even Davout had been
unable to retrieve his blunders. His one great merit was
his docility: he allowed his all-powerful brother to quash
his American marriage and arrange for a more suitable
one with Princess Catherine of Württemberg. In 1815
he rushed to the support of the returned Emperor. But
thereafter he showed little interest in dynastic claims. As
early as 1830 he would have been delighted to play the
easy and profitable role of "historical monument," which
he achieved only in 1848. He thought that his nephew's
harebrained escapades spoiled the chances of his coming
to profitable terms with Louis-Philippe, and he did not
conceal his anger. But he was ready for a gamble; just as
he had backed the precarious regime of the Hundred
Days, he came out in favor of the *Coup d'État* when its
success was still uncertain: of his own accord, he rode
behind his nephew on the fateful morning of December 2. Napoleon III invariably spoke of the old sport,
the Prodigal Uncle, with affection and respect. He

would praise his mature experience, his never-failing sanity. So the "sterling qualities" of King Jerome, along with the "virtues" of the Empress Josephine, came to be accepted at the Tuileries as familiar and polite fictions. With a very slight effort, the courtiers managed to keep a straight face.

Mathilde, born in 1820, had been a handsome and spirited young girl; she attained, in her middle years, an ample Juno-like beauty. Louis-Napoleon's cousinly affection for her burst into love before she was sixteen, and a marriage between them was seriously considered. But King Jerome, furious at the Strasbourg adventure, broke off the romance. The union of his daughter with Prince Anatole Demidoff suited his book—and his pocketbook—considerably better. But if the Russian prince was of immense wealth, he was also of a disreputable character. After five years (1840–45), Mathilde obtained from the Tsar a separation, with a very handsome settlement.

When her cousin became President, she did the honors of the Élysée for him; but their idyl did not revive. Many have regretted it: in looks and spirit, she would have made a very fine empress. She was a born extrovert; perhaps her zest for life would have assuaged his obstinate melancholy. But in all likelihood the union would have been a stormy one. Once she said: "How I wish I could break his head, to find out what goes on inside!" Historians echo the wish: Napoleon III is a hard nut to crack. For national and dynastic reasons—with a slight admixture of personal pique—she vehemently opposed her cousin's marriage with "the Spaniard."

She found consolation in an alliance, unofficial but tacitly acknowledged, with handsome Count de Nie-

werkerke. Thanks to her, he became Superintendent of
Fine Arts—a position to which Louis-Napoleon's old
friend Count d'Orsay had been appointed a few days
before his death. There Mathilde was in her element:
she loved the society of artists and writers. They in return liked her company, and not purely for snobbish reasons. Sainte-Beuve's correspondence with her (published
as *Letters to the Princess*, as though she alone bore that
title) is an illuminating document. There was no glamour about Sainte-Beuve: not a brilliant creative writer,
a rancorous soul in a graceless frame. But she understood the supreme gift of intelligence in the disenchanted old critic. She forced him into the Senate (Napoleon III did not even know to which paper he was
contributing his famous *Monday Talks*); in that dignified mausoleum he alone with Mérimée and Prince
Napoleon let in a scandalous whiff of independent
thought. For all her modern ideas, Princess Mathilde
remained—pardonably—a devotee of Napoleon I. She
left a card *pour prendre congé* on her valued friend
Taine because, in his *Origins of Contemporary France*,
he had deviated from the strict Napoleonic orthodoxy.
In that simple faith she died in 1904.

Mathilde's brother, Napoleon, was called *Plonplon*
in his childhood. The nickname was revived by his
soldiers in the Crimea; with no touch of affectionate
familiarity, for he was far from popular. The opposition
took up the absurd name: Plonplon he remained to the
end, just as Napoleon III, for obscure reasons, remained
Badinguet.

Louis-Napoleon, the elder by fourteen years, always
felt for his volcanic young cousin an affection that was
fraternal and quasi-paternal. He had helped the boy with

his lessons; when he reached power, he gave the young man unlimited opportunities. At twenty-seven Prince Napoleon was Ambassador to Spain; at thirty-two he commanded a division. He was commissioner general of the great Paris Expositions in 1855 and 1867; he headed an army corps in Italy; he was editor in chief of the first Emperor's enormous correspondence; he was entrusted with the ministry for Algeria and the colonies. This was not sheer nepotism on the Emperor's part: he was sincerely convinced of his cousin's outstanding abilities, and he wanted to train for leadership the reckless young man who might be his successor.

The sentiments of Prince Napoleon toward his imperial cousin were, to put it charitably, ambivalent, and ambivalence is a perilous state of mind. Perhaps the curse of Plonplon's career is that he shared with John Gordon, the San Francisco watchmaker, a striking resemblance to the great Napoleon. Even earlier than his uncle's, his features lost their Cæsar-like sharpness: he was described as "a Napoleonic medal with a smear of German lard." With the features came almost automatically the expression: Plonplon was imperious, and felt himself imperial. He mistook his savage temper for energy, and his lack of inner discipline for independence. After a brilliant start, he would grow weary of every task entrusted to him and drop it with a shrug of contempt. He could not work with others, because he was not, like his uncle, in exclusive command. A splendid alibi: it gave his unsteadiness an imperial mask. Meanwhile there was one who had the full authority that Plonplon coveted; and that one was, in his manners and speech, slow, gentle, dreamy. Plonplon despised him in his heart and spoke of him with unmeasured bitterness.

Yet we feel—and Napoleon III felt—that there were depths of affection and respect under that angry bluster.

This fundamental loyalty did not exist, of course, so far as the Empress was concerned: Plonplon, and Mathilde as well, hated Eugénie as an intruder, a for-eigner, a reactionary. The feud never was assuaged. Eugénie affected to believe that Prince Napoleon might turn into a Richard III. The battle went on after the deaths of the Emperor and the Prince Imperial: Eugénie's final victory was to win over to her side Prince Napoleon's son, Victor, so that he stood as a pretender against his own father.

The personal frustration and spite that embittered Plonplon's life were aggravated by an ideological con-flict. The most striking aspect of Bonapartism is Cæ-sarian democracy; Prince Napoleon affected to put all the stress on *democracy*. It was as a republican of the Left that he was elected to the National Assembly; in the course of his embassy to Spain, he gave vent to the most radical ideas. At the end of his career the *Appeal to the People* was more than ever the core of his creed. He did not realize the absurdity of his position. His uncle Lucien also had remained a republican at heart, but he had accepted no favor from his imperial brother. Plon-plon all too willingly took as his due his title as First Prince of the Blood, his Palais-Royal residence, his vast income, a dynastic marriage with the King of Italy's daughter. He lived in the naïve faith that democracy could not fail to choose a Napoleon; and that, among the Napoleons, it should pick out the one who looked most Napoleonic. As a matter of fact, the democrats never took him seriously. When his name was mentioned on September 4, 1870, it evoked only a sneer. When in the 1880's there was in France a vague and turbulent fascist movement, it selected as its leader not Prince Napoleon, but a plebeian second-rate general, Boulanger.

What Plonplon did not realize is that Bonapartism means *balance*. No reaction, no revolution. Order first of all, but order as the condition of progress. Democracy, and even social democracy, unlimited, but with the vested interests reassured. It would have been excellent for the Empire if the two tendencies in Bonapartism had been clearly represented in the imperial family: the Emperor's cousin on the left, the Emperor's wife on the right. Unfortunately, both were narrow in their respective creeds because both were narrow of heart: haughty, spiteful, and far less clever than they imagined. So their contrast became a violent conflict. Instead of enriching the regime, it exposed it to violent jerks.

Yet this damaging portrait of the "outcast Cæsar," as his friend the brilliant journalist Edmond About called him, would be a caricature if we did not recognize that there were elements of greatness in the man. They were marred, not, as he thought, by unjust outward circumstances, but by an inner flaw. In everything he undertook, he showed spasmodic ability. He shook the sleepy Senate with his uncouth but undeniable eloquence. Like his sister, he sought the society of artists and writers. He even corresponded with P. J. Proudhon, the great socialist thinker, perhaps the greatest of them all, who had been called "a one-man Terror." He won a certain degree of consideration from George Sand, whose heart was ardent for all generous causes, and whose mind, when the romantic storm was over, was surprisingly clear. His greatest title to our respect is that he was accepted as a member in good standing in the Magny dinner group,

which comprised such men as Sainte-Beuve, Taine, and
Renan.

Each of the characters sketched above had some definite contact with the Emperor. From these contacts we
may hope to discern, if not his figure, at least his shadow.
And in that indirect approach, feminine figures may be
of commanding importance.

Cherchez la femme is not the key to the Second Empire, and I have no desire to indulge in *chronique
scandaleuse*. But it is a fact that the most sedate historians
cannot ignore: Napoleon III was an inveterate amorist.
His list of conquests is paltry compared with that of
Don Juan Tenorio. But it is remarkable in its range,
from an actress of genius like Rachel and a great lady
like Countess Walewska to a mere grisette like Marguerite Bellanger.

It is not my purpose to exculpate him: I am merely
writing a historical footnote to the Kinsey report. Re-
alistically—that is, cynically—it is a fact that chastity
is not the first virtue in a sovereign: Henri IV was a
better king than Louis XVI. We must add that, as a
rule, Napoleon III kept his love affairs and his political
endeavors on strictly separate ledgers. Miss Howard
helped him, but he was not influenced by her. Cavour
sent him the Countess de Castiglione to be an agent for
the Italian cause. She was a magnificent young beast of
prey, shameless, rapacious, and stupid. Napoleon, nothing loath, pocketed the handsome bribe; but it did not
deflect him in the least from his own line of action,
which, ironically, happened to be the same as Cavour's.
The only fault of Napoleon III as a statesman in his relations with women was the same as Louis XVI's: his

uxoriousness. The worst of husbands from the private point of view, he was also too good a husband for the best interests of France: in the last years of his reign he gave the Empress a share in the counsels of the state for which she was congenitally unfit. That was, to a great extent, the ransom of his manifold sins. So, indirectly, by giving Eugénie a grievance, and thereby enhancing her power, Marguerite Bellanger and her likes contributed to the decline of the Empire.

The prolonged Howard episode might well tempt a romancer. She and the prince met in London, it seems through Count d'Orsay. She was a lady with a past of impenetrable shadiness. When Louis-Napoleon knew her, she had climbed from the depths of the underworld to the sunniest reaches of the demimonde. Catering to the quality trade, she had already amassed a fortune. She was—a rarely acknowledged phenomenon under Victoria's reign—a hetaira like the Aspasia of Pericles, a courtesan whose wit and practical sense matched her beauty. Louis-Napoleon squandered his money on her, but it proved a sound investment. She had listened to his tales of imperial grandeur as Desdemona listened to Othello. She believed in him, and at the right moment she backed him with the utmost generosity. No one will ever know to what extent the tainted gold of Miss Howard helped the French make up their minds in 1848 and 1851.

She expected her reward: if not a throne, at least the position of an official favorite. During the journeys of the Prince-President throughout France, she accompanied him as a carelessly kept secret. Her hour sounded when Eugénie appeared. Less than a week before the imperial marriage she received the estate and title of

Countess de Beauregard. Thereafter she ceased from troubling—not without assistance from the police. She died of cancer in 1865.

The new Emperor was forty-four. For the two preceding decades there had been many matrimonial rumors concerning him: with his cousin Mathilde, with Queen Maria of Portugal, with maidens of the British upper class. He probably had in mind, like his uncle, a dynastic union. There were not a few eligibles in the first and second parts of the *Almanach de Gotha*. Through Eugène and Stéphanie de Beauharnais, through Jerome, through Bernadotte, the Bonaparte connection had already many links with the most illustrious houses: after all, Napoleon I was able to refer to the Emperor of Austria as "Papa Francis," and to Louis XVI as "my uncle." It was therefore with consternation that the imperial circle heard of Napoleon III's engagement to Eugenia de Montijo.

Frankly, he had been caught. Not, as his family broadly hinted, by the wiles of cosmopolitan adventuresses: the term would not quite fit the Countess de Montijo y Teba, and even less her daughters. It is true that, flitting from pleasure resort to pleasure resort, they displayed an aristocratic freedom that the more sedate elements in French society found suspicious. It is true that the old countess was a colorful character; she was too vivid even for the gaudiest of empires, and was not allowed permanently to grace the Tuileries. But their titles were genuine enough: a long list of them, including three *grandezas* of Spain. And although Eugénie, much traveled and twenty-six, was hardly a naïve debutante, her conduct had been, and was to remain, above reproach. She admired the Emperor: so did Elizabeth

Barrett Browning. His vertiginous ascent had made him
the most romantic figure of the time. She was deeply
flattered by his marked attentions. But she did not deliberately plan to force herself upon him.

   Napoleon III was caught in a trap of his own making.
He had reached that noonday of life in which a devil
lurks (*a demonio meridiano libera nos, Domine*): it is
the late, the last hour for a consuming and rejuvenating
passion. He had no thought at first but of a spirited flirtation, at most of an affair. Eugénie was an aristocrat, a
pious Catholic, of a cold temperament, and with experience enough to play her cards well: a formidable array
of defenses. Her refusal even to understand Napoleon's
advances struck him as evidence of the rarest virtue. The
court and, above all, the imperial family saw the peril.
Their open hostility offended Eugénie, who haughtily
prepared to retire. This move challenged Napoleon's
sense of chivalry: a pure girl had been insulted under his
roof and through his fault. It roused also his resentment
against interference: after all, was he not the master?
And her beauty was without a peer in that golden age
of fair women: chroniclers gloated, and scholars dry as
dust still gloat, over the pure oval of her face, her eyes
of sapphire, her Venetian hair, and those sloping shoulders she so generously displayed. On January 30, 1853
they were married at Notre-Dame, in a gorgeous ceremony that amounted to a coronation.

   In those miraculous years it looked as though Napoleon could do nothing wrong. Against the dire fore-
bodings of his family, his very rashness increased his
popularity. A self-made Emperor who marries for love:
this perfected a career that had been sheer romance. And
in the imperial pageant the Empress played her part

well: she took lessons from Rachel, as Napoleon I had
taken lessons from Talma. If Princess Pauline Metternich, the ugliest, merriest madcap in the hectic days of
the regime, refused to recognize Eugénie as "a real empress," it is striking that Victoria and her consort, Albert
the Good, accepted her at once as an intimate friend.

She was, of course, a model of lavish elegance: Eugénie styles are still periodically revived. But she was
more than the most gorgeous mannequin in the capital
of *haute couture*. She could show simple courage. She
visited the sick during a cholera epidemic. When Orsini's
bombs killed and wounded men of her escort, and her
dress was bespattered with blood, she did not flinch. In
the first years of her reign she took no part in politics,
and was by no means committed to reaction. Sincerely
pious, she had not been reared in a somber clerical atmosphere. Her father had been an *afrancesado*, one of
those Spanish liberals who had rallied to King Joseph because they hoped that the Napoleonic system would turn
Spain into a modern nation. Among her mother's friends
were Prosper Mérimée and "Monsieur Beyle," better
remembered as Stendhal. Both had been kind to the little
Spanish girls, the future Duchess of Alba and the future
Empress of the French; and Eugénie felt for both a life-
long respectful affection. It is odd to think of her reading
a lesson in tolerance to an imperial tribunal; yet when
Baudelaire's *Flowers of Evil* was condemned in 1857,
she offered to pay his fine. The sum was trifling, but the
gesture was elegant. She was, in those early years, neither
la femme futile nor *la femme fatale* that her enemies were
so fiercely to denounce.

To her intimates, however, she was known to be
vivacious rather than clever; incapable of sustained think-

ing; dropping every book after a cursory glance; an exceeding worshipper of her own beauty; capricious and quick to anger, with a cold sharpness in her irritation which wounded her well-wishers. She commanded reluctant admiration from the very first; and in her interminable widowhood she attracted universal respect. But I have seen no sign in contemporary correspondences (even Mérimée's) or in family traditions that she could inspire tenderness, that odd spontaneous tribute which the people's heart denied Marie Antoinette and gave so gratuitously to Josephine.

These were the closest associates of the Emperor. Faults and virtues, he had much in common with them. There is a period style that blurs individual traits: these, and the sovereign at their head, were all *Second Empire*. Yet we are aware of a difference: a difference so profound that it sets him wholly apart. And that quality, so strange in his sophisticated, cynical, glittering world, was deep, modest, unremitting kindness. Of this we have testimonies from men who were not blinded by Bonapartist faith—Mérimée, Victor Duruy, the historian, Émile Ollivier, a leader of the republican opposition, and most striking of all, perhaps, Louis Pasteur. That man who lived among the superb, that man who was so far from good, whose formal faith was so mottled and hard to define, that man had the one essential Christian virtue, *misericordia*. What baffles history is this: that the innermost truth about Napoleon III should at the same time be so plain and so outrageously paradoxical.

CHAPTER FIVE

THE ARBITER OF EUROPE
1854–1859

THE BASILICA of St. Geneviève, in Paris, became
the Panthéon in 1790, St. Geneviève again in 1814, the
Panthéon once more in 1830, St. Geneviève for the
third time in 1851, the Panthéon (until further notice)
in 1885. Its decoration mirrors these vicissitudes. It is
at the same time patriotic and religious. The visitor can
see St. Denys picking up his severed head, St. Geneviève
watching over the sleeping city, St. Joan of Arc in her
martyrdom. But instead of an altar, there is a monument
to the Revolution. Back of it, in the apse, we find a vast
composition by Édouard Detaille: *On to Glory!* a
cavalry charge storming the very heavens, or, for the
Voltairian scoffer, a circus parade *in excelsis*. The mind
of Napoleon III was such a Panthéon: Catholic and
monarchical tradition leading up to the Revolution; and,
in the most conspicuous place, the apotheosis of military
glamour.

This, of course, gives a distorted view both of
French history and of the Emperor's mind. He was profoundly, as he professed to be, a man of peace. A Saint-
Simonian in spirit, he aspired to be a Captain of Industry, not a brutal conqueror. He had had some military
training, but not a military career. When, in the Italian
campaign, he saw for the first time the horrors of the
battlefield, his humane heart rebelled. But he was a
French sovereign: the military tradition—Louis XIV,
the Revolution, Napoleon—had taken hold of him and

would not let him go. It may be obvious to us that the age of Louis XIV was great for its cultural achievements, and that its bellicose ventures were flaws in its glory; that the Principles of 1789 outshone and outlasted the marvelous triumphs of the republican armies; that Napoleon's conquests were but a phantasmagoria, while his Civil Code was a reality. But the epic romance of war has an indestructible appeal. In the popular mind, there is no substitute for victory.

The Second Empire was an industrial regime with military trappings. In this respect, Bismarckian Germany aped Napoleonic France. But with a difference: the Germans took their war pageantry with deadly earnestness, and army-worship became their national sin. France's affection for her soldiers was tempered with a smile. A hundred years ago war was still a romance of bravery and adventure, but as a tournament rather than as a quest. If the armed forces were cheered, it was as "the team."

Clemenceau was guided by his recollection of the Second Empire when he said: "War is too serious a thing to be entrusted to the generals." This, of course, must be accepted as it was uttered, with a grin. We should not exaggerate the frivolousness of the military under Napoleon III. Pélissier was probably a match for any of the marshals of Napoleon I except Masséna and Davout. Mac-Mahon, Canrobert, Bosquet, were devoted to their profession, modest at heart, heroically brave, and adequate to any task except independent command. Niel was a forward-looking organizer. Even the men whose shadows darken the beginning and the end of the regime—Saint-Arnaud and Bazaine—had their brief hour of deserved success. But compared with

the financiers, the engineers, the scientists, the philoso-
phers, the poets, the artists, of that truly brilliant era,
they were second-rate. Under a genius, they might have
been adequate instruments. But Napoleon III, conscientious and well informed in military matters, did not
possess the mastery of details, the flash of intuition, the
power of immediate decision, which enabled his uncle
to win six campaigns out of twelve. When, at Magenta,
Frossard brought him the news: "Sire, what a glorious
victory!" the ingenuous victor confessed: "A victory,
is it? And I was going to order a retreat!" If, in actual
command, he did win the Battle of Solferino—his
glorious hour—it was chiefly thanks to his opponent,
Francis Joseph.

The armies of the Second Empire were perhaps the
last to have *style*. There was in them something of the
Froissart glamour: the shining armor, the pennon, and
the plume. There was also a blend of humor and elegance, of bravado and faultless courage, *à la* Cyrano,
à la d'Artagnan: an afterglow of gay romance in an age
of dingy realism. Of this Second Empire *Beau Sabreur*
type, there is no better model than the Marquis de Galliffet, a wit of pungent, Gallic raciness, the hero of duels
and affairs, fancy-dress balls and theatricals, the tireless
leader of counter-guerrillas in Mexico, and, at Sedan, the
man who, hurling his Algerian light horse against the
Prussian lines, wrenched from King William the cry:
"Oh! The brave men!"

But it is exceedingly dangerous for adult nations to
play soldiers. The military parade of the Second Empire
filled Europe with misgivings. From the day of the
Coup d'État to the outbreak of the Franco-Prussian War,
England lived in dread lest Napoleon should seize

Belgium, and Prussia feared for her Rhine provinces. Even if the clangor of arms and the blare of trumpets had not made Europe uneasy, it would have encouraged in France the most dangerous temptation that can assail a country: a craving for prestige. France, under the Second Empire, was good-humored, with a touch of irony, sociable, hospitable: none of that grim unhuman mask that the Nazis imposed upon Germany. But still, France was "the Great Nation," the strongest military power on earth, and her fiat was law. From 1866 to 1870 it was the opposition that taunted the government for its lack of spirit; the war that engulfed the regime was started on the merest question of prestige. It is very ancient wisdom that "pride goeth before destruction, and a haughty spirit before a fall."

Here we find most clearly expressed the first contradiction inherent in the Second Empire. Napoleon III had poured into the Napoleonic Legend a totally new conception, far more generous than anything that ever crossed his uncle's mind: still, he was the heir of the Legend, and the Legend is inseparable from power and glory. The shade of the Great Emperor was constantly at his elbow, tempting him: "With the principles of 1789 as your guides, the Great Nation solid behind you, a well-disciplined army in your hand, who could stand against you?"

Napoleon III did resist the most obvious temptations. In 1840, before the Chamber of Peers, and again in his speeches as President, he had stood against the Vienna *Diktat*, so bitterly resented by the French. Thus he challenged the established order, dear to the Metternich-Guizot type of mind, and this challenge carried a threat of war. But on his accession he made it plain that he

did not intend to start a crusade against the whole
Vienna settlement. The restoration of the Empire, and
his assuming the title of Napoleon *the Third*, symbolically destroyed the hated treaties: he was satisfied.
There was in him no spirit of petty revenge. It was England that had finally humbled Napoleon at Waterloo,
England that had caged him in St. Helena, but a firm
and cordial alliance with England was the core of his
foreign policy. The French felt the martyrdom of Poland as a personal wrong. In 1848, riotous mobs had
urged a war for the immediate liberation of Poland. This
feeling remained strong during the next two decades. It
was perhaps the only point on which the Empress and
Prince Napoleon saw eye to eye. Even without the active support of England, if all the oppressed peoples
throughout Europe had been called to arms, victory over
Russia, Austria, and Prussia combined was not un-
thinkable. But the risk was enormous and the cost appalling. With a heavy heart, Napoleon III refused to
stir.

What frightened Europe about Napoleon III was
that he had a dynamic faith. His motto was not *Quieta
non movere*—in plain English, *Let sleeping dogs lie*—
but *Injustices need not be eternal*. He had been brought
up in an atmosphere of romantic democracy: the nations are "not thrones and crowns, but men." The peoples have a right to assert themselves against masters not
of their own choosing—whether privileged classes or
foreign oppressors. In the thirties and forties, nationalism
and democracy were one, and both had a religious
tinge. "God save the People!" sang Ebenezer Elliott,
the Corn-Law Rhymer; "God and the People," said
Mazzini, and this was the very formula of Napoleon's

power: *Emperor by the Grace of God and the Will of the People.* He was sincere in repudiating any thought of conquest: it was France's mission to liberate, not to enslave. Self-determination, ascertained through a plebiscite, was his goal; then free nations could live as happy neighbors. The kinship between his "doctrine of nationalities" and Wilsonism is undeniable, although Woodrow Wilson never acknowledged so embarrassing a forerunner.

But here we find another contradiction in that strangely compounded regime. Napoleon's policy was democratic. As such, it menaced not merely the territorial *status quo* and the tremulous balance among the European powers: it imperiled the even more tremulous balance between the classes and the masses. It was "an appeal to the people," and that, in the eyes of all the autocrats, the Pope as well as the dynasts, meant revolution. For certain minds, it is the nature of all holy causes to be subversive; for others, revolution means the stirring of turbid depths. Now Napoleon III, a revolutionary at heart, had "saved Society," "stemmed the Red tide," restored Order, bolstered Property. The Tsar and the Catholic hierarchy had heartily approved of the *Coup d'État.*

According to all "realistic" historians, Napoleon III was "woefully disinterested"; and they blame him roundly for preferring the golden haze of principles to the plain facts of national interest. He welcomed the idea of a united Italy, a united Germany, although it would jeopardize France's predominance in continental Europe: the moral gain, to his mind, would more than compensate for the material loss. He wanted no privilege for France. But he believed that France, no less than

other nations, was entitled to her *rights*. And unfor-
tunately those rights, for him and for three generations of
Frenchmen, implied the so-called "natural frontiers," the
Alps and the Rhine.

By imperceptible degrees the French had worked
themselves up into the delusion that for a thousand years
they had yearned and travailed for these "lost" natural
frontiers. That ideal—a curious case of false memory, of
an artificially induced tradition—triumphed against the
advice of Carnot in 1795. Then the Rhine became "the
frontier of liberty." Half a century later Victor Hugo
was urging Germany to restore to France "what God
Himself had given her, the Rhine." How easy, how
tempting it is to forge God's signature! And it was long
before the reign of Napoleon III that Becker and Alfred de Musset had hurled at each other angry and extremely mediocre poems about the *German Rhine*.

It must be remembered that a hundred years ago the
notion of a French left bank of the Rhine was not so
absurd as it was in 1919, or as it may seem today. The
Rhinelanders had been tolerably well satisfied under
French rule from 1795 to 1814, and their Prussian
"liberators" complained of their extreme coolness. There
was no actual "Germany" to command loyalty; the Emperor in Vienna was more remote, more shadowy, less
enlightened than the Emperor in Paris. The upper
classes spoke French by choice. As for Belgium, when
seceding from the Netherlands in 1830, it had desired
incorporation with France; it was only the pressure of
Europe, and particularly of England, that had imposed a
compromise solution, neutrality and independence under
a Saxe-Coburg-Gotha, who married a daughter of

Louis-Philippe. French opinion did not fully realize that, in a few decades, a great change had taken place: by 1852 the Belgians felt themselves Belgians, the Rhinelanders Germans. The historical spirit should be the sense of constant, and at times rapid, evolution. From the German point of view, the Second Empire was coveting, not merely Luxembourg or Sarrebruck, but Trèves, Mayence, Cologne. There could be no genuine peace until that nightmare was exorcised.

Thus the man whose principles were so lofty, and whose temper was so kind, turned into a disturbing element, a universal menace, all the more pervasive because of its vagueness. To his fellow rulers, the impenetrable eyes of the French Emperor became lakes of unfathomable deceit. His opportunistic tacking was interpreted as deviousness. When he spoke in clearest tones, he was not believed: his words were scanned for their hidden implications. When he remained silent, it proved that "the Sphinx of the Tuileries" was nursing mysterious designs. Queen Victoria, who liked him personally, was never able to trust him. In such an ambiguous position, even the bluntest, most straightforward man would appear as a baleful schemer. After all, he had been a conspirator until he ascended the throne: why not a crowned conspirator? By the dispassionate historian, the *Coup d'État* may be accepted as the legitimate consequence of his popular election in December 1848; but it was none the less a technical breach of the law, an act of force prepared in secrecy. Conservation? Democracy? Personal ambition? Bluster? No one knew what Napoleon would do next, or why. So the sovereign who in the depths of his being was a Woodrow Wilson, only less smug and of a warmer heart, created the impression of a Hitler.

In 1812 Russia had "saved Europe" from Napo-leonic Jacobinism; the Holy Alliance was the prolonged shadow of that victory. In 1849 Russia had rescued Austria, citadel of conservatism in central Europe. Tsar Nicholas I believed himself to be the divinely appointed defender of order, and in that capacity he had nodded approval of the *Coup d'État*. But he balked at the res-toration of the French Empire: for that meant the destruction of the Vienna settlement, that charter of the Counter-Revolution. So he haggled over his recog-nition of the new regime. Finally he saved his face by ad-dressing the French Emperor as "his good friend" in-stead of "his brother." Napoleon smiled courteously: "Brothers are given to us; but we pick out our friends." This slight friction left no trace: there was little vanity and no rancor in the Emperor's character.

But there was an issue deeper than the terms of rec-ognition, deeper than the letter of the treaties of 1815: Europe would never breathe freely until the formidable pressure exerted by Russia was removed. This did not mean war, not even a cold war. But it meant a contest for influence. It would have been easy for Napoleon to join a Continental block of reactionary empires: some of his advisers urged him in that direction. He chose Western liberalism, because he was a progressive at heart, and because he knew, liked, and trusted England.

Conservatism, for the Tsar, did not necessarily mean preserving the territorial *status quo*. He believed in ex-panding the area of order—that is, his own dominions— at the cost of the Ottoman Empire. It was then that the

Turk was first called "the sick man of Europe," and Russia hinted to England that it would be well to divide the spoils ahead of the inevitable collapse. England, thinking first of all of her supremacy in the Mediterranean and of the roads to India, demurred. So the Near Eastern problem flared up once more, as it had in 1827–9 and in 1840; as it was to break out again in 1877–8, 1897, 1913. Even in the middle decades of the twentieth century, whatever degree of peace prevails in that troubled region is but a fragile film.

The specific origin of the crisis that confronted the new Emperor of the French was insignificant enough: obscure squabbles between Latin (Catholic) and Greek Orthodox monks about the custody of certain holy places in Jerusalem. But back of this minor problem stood a much larger issue. If Russia intervened in support of the Greek Orthodox, she might ultimately claim a protectorate over them throughout the Ottoman Empire; then the greater part of the Balkans would turn into Russian satellites and the rule of the Turks in Europe would become purely nominal.

This issue was forced by the Tsar. In February 1853 he sent Prince Menshikov as his special envoy to Constantinople. With an escort so impressive as to give a foretaste of invasion, Menshikov attempted to cajole or coerce the Sublime Porte into agreement. So far, both England and France had played a very cautious hand. England, as a Protestant power, cared very little about the ecclesiastical aspect of the problem, but she balked at the enormous expansion of the Russian claims. After more than three months, Menshikov had to retire baffled, uttering vague threats. The Tsar thought that it was time to "discuss from a position of strength," and in-

vaded the Danubian principalities, Moldavia and Wal-
lachia. Thereupon the British sent war vessels to the
Dardanelles, and a French force joined them.

No one in France, from the sovereign to the most
humble peasant, had the slightest desire for war. There
was among the French no hatred of Russia, no deep-
seated pro-Turkish sentiment, no enthusiasm for the
British alliance. Napoleon, well aware of this state of
mind, was still doing his best to avert an open conflict.
It was the opposition, now in exile, that was bellicose:
Victor Hugo poured contempt on Napoleon's "coward-
ice." Even Prince Albert, so elaborately "good," in a
private letter to his friend Stockmar, denounced the
"appeasement" policy of the French government. Again
it was Russia's aggressiveness that ended the long incer-
titude. A Russian fleet found the Turkish navy at Sinope
in the Black Sea and destroyed it utterly. Unless England
and France made a decisive move, Russia would be
supreme, not in the Balkans merely, but in the whole
Levant. Even then there were a number of hesitant steps.
It was not until March 12, 1854 that England and
France allied themselves with Turkey; and the formal
declaration of war came only on March 28. Thus the
Christian West was uniting with the Infidels against
Orthodox Russia: Clio is a ironic muse. Napoleon III's
sole consolation, in asking the legislative body for war
credits, was to reaffirm his forward-looking principles in
very noble terms, which are still valid today.

The war into which great nations had stumbled was
conducted on every side with incredible incompetence.
The British revealed once more that genius for muddling
of which they are so inordinately proud, and in the first
months the French were hardly better off. In the second

year, however, thanks to a large extent to Florence
Nightingale, the supplies and sanitary equipment of the
British became less inadequate, while the French could
show no comparable improvement. Of the hundred
thousand lives lost in that absurd campaign, actual fighting accounted for only ten thousand. No wonder Richard Cobden, when his little boy asked him: "What do
those letters C-R-I-M-E-A mean?" answered with in-
tense conviction: "My son: A CRIME." There were
heroic episodes, but two famous phrases sum them up:
Tennyson's admission: "Some one had blunder'd," and
General Bosquet's dubious praise: "It is magnificent,
but it is not war." Seldom has mankind offered a purer
example of conspicuous waste.

An old diplomatic cliché describes the eternal contest
between Russia and England as "the duel of the ele-
phant and the whale." It was impossible for Russia to
strike at the Western allies; she could only wait for their
attack, and endeavor to hurl them back into the sea. The
allies could not reach any vital part of the Russian Empire: amphibian operations in the Baltic were merely a
diversion. But the vast distances that were Russia's best
protection were also her chief handicap. Paradoxically,
it was more difficult for Russia than for the allies to supply their respective troops in the Crimea: the sea af-
forded a much better highway than could be found in
the quagmires of central Russia. So, by tacit consent, the
fate of the war was linked with that of a single city, the
naval base of Sebastopol.

Saint-Arnaud had died—heart and cholera; Canrobert had failed, and remained as a divisional commander;
Pélissier, with fine soldierly indifference for mere human
lives, ordered the final assault. At one moment the tre-

mendous conflict narrowed down to the possession of one key position, the Malakoff Tower, captured by Mac-Mahon. When the Russians could no longer defend the crumbling walls, they scuttled the ships, blew up the ammunition dumps, set the city on fire, and retired in good order (September 8, 1855).

Had Nicholas lived, his fanatical pride would not have accepted this local defeat as final. But he had died on March 2, and Alexander II was less unbending. Austria, "astounding the world with her ingratitude," had already joined, although not as a belligerent, the enemies of Russia, that Russia which had saved her only six years before. When Austria presented a peace offer as an ultimatum, the Tsar agreed to preliminary conditions, which were ratified in Paris on March 30, 1856.

This dismal tale of diplomatic and military blundering is part of European history, and not primarily of Napoleon's personal life. For many months he kept champing at the bit. What the campaign needed was a single command, with a daring leader; and who was better qualified than the hero of Strasbourg, Boulogne, and the *Coup d'État?* The thought appalled the officers in the field: it was bad enough to have Prince Napoleon at the head of a division. England was horrified: if the Emperor assumed command, the British would be reduced to the position of auxiliaries. The Emperor was told that his life was too precious, and the regime as yet too frail, to run such a tragic risk. The sovereign was the prisoner of his own greatness. So, twirling his right mustache and chewing the left, he submitted to safety and comfort.

Napoleon III, in the first decade of his reign, was

miraculously lucky. This war, so patently useless and so
unpopular, strengthened his regime: nations rally to the
flag, even in a questionable cause. Actual conditions in
the trenches were squalid; but the Orient still had a romantic glamour—although this time the crusaders were
on the wrong side. France, in spite of temporary economic difficulties, felt that she had entered upon an era
of prosperity; the Paris Exposition of 1855 was an un-
qualified success. Sovereign and people were brought
closer together than they had been under the Restoration or Louis-Philippe.

Above all, the war turned England from a critical
and acrimonious neighbor into a full-fledged ally. This
collaboration was sealed by state visits: Prince Albert
at Boulogne (September 5, 1854), Napoleon and Eugénie at Windsor and in London (April 1855), Victoria and Albert at Saint-Cloud and Paris (August
1855). Unexpectedly, the royal and imperial pairs
took to each other at once. Albert was delighted with
the German aspects of Napoleon's baffling personality:
they swapped poetical quotations and students' ditties.
Victoria was won over by his gentleness and courtesy.
Beneath the obvious charm of the Empress, the Queen
discerned womanly qualities that were not fully revealed
to the outer world until her downfall and exile. In spite
of her inveterate pro-Germanism and her strong disap-
proval of the Emperor's methods, Victoria remained
loyal to the memory of those halcyon days; and she was
a close friend of Eugénie to the very last. The French
people were far less Anglophilic than their sovereign:
veterans of Waterloo wondered what "the Other," the
Uncle, would feel about this junketing with "perfidious

Albion." But the royal pair were hailed by the Parisian
crowds with a courtesy that was a very tolerable substitute for enthusiasm.

So the monumental blunder of the Crimean War
ended preposterously, in a triumph. The Peace Congress, to which many neutrals had been invited, met in
Paris from February 25 to March 30, 1856, and was
imperially entertained. There was no *Diktat*, no "un-
conditional surrender": the spirit was that of honorable
opponents shaking hands as soon as the contest is over.
The war left no rancor: Morny, as Ambassador to the
court of St. Petersburg, removed the last traces of ill
feeling. Russia had suffered a setback; but, as early as
1870, the disabilities imposed by the Treaty of Paris
were removed.

Napoleon III attempted to turn the Peace Congress
into his favorite device: a Council of Europe. He
sounded England about the possibilities of peaceful territorial readjustments. England, always practical-minded,
believed that wars could best be averted in the approved,
time-honored way: by muddling into them. On two
points Napoleon's desire for constructive action was
satisfied. An International Commission was created to
supervise navigation on the Danube, and principles of
maritime law were adopted: privateering was abolished,
the rights of neutrals were reaffirmed, the conditions of
a valid blockade defined.

Perhaps it was a fluke, perhaps a fleeting vision of
a happier age, but in March 1856 the humanitarian
Emperor, trusted rather than feared, stood as the arbiter
of Europe. On the 16th of March, Palm Sunday, the
Empress was delivered of a son. A salute of one hundred and one guns announced the birth of the Prince

Imperial, and Paris was delirious. So swiftly, so inevitably had the prisoner of Ham and the exile in London
ascended to the pinnacle.

It was a principle with Napoleon III that *nationalities*, ethnic groups with a common language and a common tradition, had the right to become *nations*. In the
case of Italy this conviction assumed the ardor of a personal faith: he was an Italian patriot. So were, one hundred years ago, a number of very loyal Englishmen.
Patriotism is not necessarily jealous and exclusive: there
were many ardent "Polish patriots" among the French
throughout the nineteenth century.

Why was Napoleon III such a good Italian? Perhaps because his uncle Eugène had been a very acceptable Viceroy of Italy; perhaps because Rome was the
gathering-point of the exiled Bonapartes. We have seen
that, in 1831, the two sons of Louis had taken part in
an insurrection ultimately intended to liberate the whole
of Italy. So, in this case, principles and sentiments were
in accord; and they were not in manifest antagonism
with French interests. A united Italy would be, not a
rival, but a steadfast ally. Napoleon III nursed, among
his vaguer dreams, the idea of a "Latin Union." The
hegemony of France in such a regional understanding
was at that time beyond challenge.

No romantic explanation therefore is needed to account for Napoleon III's determination: neither a secret oath he might have sworn as a youthful *carbonaro*
nor Orsini's bomb (January 14, 1858) nor the dazzling
young charms of Countess de Castiglione. Napoleon
simply believed in the Italian cause, and he thought
that Providence expected his co-operation.

Austria was the obstacle. She held the Lombard-Venetian kingdom outright; she controlled the duchies of Tuscany, Parma, and Modena; her influence was great at the Papal court, although it was French troops that were guarding the Holy City. It was plain that Austria, proudest of the old dynasties, would brook no curtailment of her dominant position. Oppressive force would have to be removed by force.

The indispensable instrument was Piedmont (technically the Kingdom of Sardinia). During the Crimean War, Napoleon had welcomed a Piedmontese contingent, so that the country might be assured of a place at the council table. He had hinted at the possibility of broaching the Italian question at the Paris Congress, but he had been rebuffed. Now he quietly prepared for intervention.

On July 20, 1858, at Plombières, a spa in eastern France, he had a secret interview with a bespectacled gentleman by the name of Giuseppe Benso, better known to history as Count Camillo Cavour, Premier and Minister of Foreign Affairs for H. M. Victor Emmanuel II. On December 10 a formal, but still secret, treaty was agreed upon between the two countries. On January 1, 1859, Napoleon III publicly expressed regret that the relations between Austria and France were not satisfactory. On January 30 Prince Napoleon married Princess Clotilde of Savoy, daughter of the King, a visible sign of the still occult alliance. The crowd hailed the bridal pair with shouts: "Down with Austria!" In Paris a pamphlet inspired by the Emperor, and a sibylline speech, gave an inkling of his intentions. The reaction in official circles was far from favorable. The ministers, and even the army leaders, advised

against a war. The conservatives, particularly the Catholics, and the Empress most of all, were ardently hostile.
German opinion rallied behind Austria. England—ed-
dies of the Orsini affair had just caused a wave of Gallo-
phobia—considered the Emperor a firebrand.

For all his apparent sluggishness, Napoleon III was
extremely sensitive to public opinion. He could probe
beneath the official surface: his prefects and his district
attorneys regularly reported to him the state of mind of
the population. He hesitated, to the great despair of
Victor Emmanuel and Cavour. Last-minute efforts were
made. Gorchakov, the Russian Chancellor, prompted
by Napoleon, proposed a European congress. England
and Prussia subscribed to the idea without enthusiasm:
a congress implied the recognition that the problem existed. Even Austria, however, accepted the proposal,
but with drastic reservations. Then, on April 20, Austria herself cut the knot: a strongly worded ultimatum
to Sardinia amounted to a declaration of war; and the
Franco-Piedmontese alliance came into action. This time
it was the Emperor's war: no one could prevent him
from heading his own troops. And it was a revolutionary
war: when he left for the front, Napoleon III was hailed
with enthusiasm by the Parisian workingmen. For the
moment, the *Coup d'État* was pardoned.

In all its civil activities the Second Empire was remarkable for its efficiency. The navy too was progressive
and well managed: so progressive that at one time the
first seagoing ironclad, *La Gloire*, could have romped
through a whole British squadron. The army, the show-
piece of the regime, was in lamentable disarray from the
Crimea to Sedan.

For this strange contradiction, three causes may be

adduced. The first was that the army lived in the aura
of Napoleon's glory: if France had succumbed in the
end, it was under the combined effort of all Europe.
This was the Grand Army of the Great Nation: what
else was needed? Such a spirit had led the successors
of Frederick the Great to Auerstädt and Jena. The second
was that the commanders under the Second Empire had
received their training under Louis-Philippe in Algerian
warfare: a second lieutenant's paradise, in which reckless courage counted for more than strategy or logistics.
The third was that Napoleon III and France wanted
peace: it was impossible to prepare, thoroughly and ostensibly, for war. When the Emperor assumed command in Italy, the army was in perfect chaos. American
veterans would describe its conditions in the pungent
phrase *snafu*.

Had the Austrians boldly marched on Turin, they
might have scored a brilliant and easy victory. But, true
to their immemorial tradition, they hesitated, crawled
forward, and hesitated again. At Magenta no one com-
prehended the situation: the Austrians had already reported victory, Berlin as well as Vienna was illuminating, when it was discovered that the French had won
after all—to their infinite surprise. As a result, Napoleon III and Victor Emmanuel II entered Milan in triumph on June 8.

But the situation, so brilliant in the official dispatches,
was in fact extremely dark. Prussia was arming, and
France had no troops left to face a menace on the Rhine.
It was urgent to end the war. But how? The French
could hardly retire as long as, nominally at least, they
were victorious. On the other hand, they could not
impose peace on the strength of a confused battle like

Magenta. Not far behind the Austrian lines stood a formidable array of fortresses to be reduced, the famous Quadrilateral: Mantua, Peschiera, Legnago, Verona. Fortunately, the Austrians again played into the hands of the French. They accepted another major contest at Solferino (June 23). It was almost as chaotic as Magenta: full of "alarums and excursions." But at the right moment Napoleon III did launch the Guard in the right direction. It was decidedly a victory, although very far from a decisive victory.

This enabled Napoleon to extricate himself from the Italian trap with all the appearances of magnanimity. Diplomacy had been fumbling in the dark: he addressed himself directly to Francis Joseph. On July 9 a cease-fire order was agreed upon. On July 10 the two sovereigns met at Villafranca. The interview was not merely correct: it was cordial. Preliminaries of peace were arranged, which were confirmed by the Treaty of Zurich on November 10. The settlement was frankly a compromise. Francis Joseph "had lost a game and paid with a province." Lombardy was ceded to France, which was free to turn it over to Piedmont. But Austria retained Venetia. The fate of the rest of Italy was left vague.

Victor Emmanuel and especially Cavour were furious at this "betrayal": had there not been a resounding promise to set Italy free from the Alps to the Adriatic? Victor Emmanuel, statesmanlike in spite of his preposterous mustaches, accepted the situation: half a loaf . . . Cavour resigned in a rage. Italian opinion turned suddenly against the halting Liberator: portraits of Orsini were displayed in windows. When Napoleon III went through Milan again, he was greeted with icy silence.

Yet it was Napoleon who could have complained
of a betrayal. He had been betrayed by England, pro-
Italian on the whole, but so jealous of the Emperor's
prestige that she refused him her diplomatic support. He
had been betrayed by Piedmont, and particularly by
Cavour. For the Italy Napoleon III envisaged was to
be free and united, but not *unitary*: a federation of Italian states, Piedmont inevitably predominating, but with
the Pope as nominal head. What Cavour had in mind
was the conquest of all Italy by Piedmont, and a cen-
tralized monarchy on the French model. Napoleon III
was probably right: the federal solution, adopted by
Germany in 1871, might have been the best for Italy.
But a French sovereign could hardly complain if a
neighboring country paid France the compliment of
imitating her institutions.

At Plombières, Napoleon and Cavour had understood themselves, but not each other. Foreshadowing
disagreement, they had thought it wiser, like Franklin
Roosevelt, to ask no *iffy* question and to cross no bridge
until they came to it. To govern is to foresee. Napoleon
had not foreseen the nature of Cavour's ambition. Cavour had not foreseen that the French ruler might understand him in time and leave him in the lurch.

But in spite of partial frustration the desperate gamble had turned out well. For Victor Emmanuel II: Tuscany, Parma, Modena, Romagna, voted their union
with Piedmont; and in a colorful epic Garibaldi gave
him Sicily, Naples, half of the Papal States. For Napoleon III: Cavour, returning to power in January
1859, paid the price: Savoy and Nice. Savoy, although
the cradle of the dynasty, was in culture a province of
France. Nice, the birthplace of Garibaldi, was on the

French side of the Alps. In accordance with Napoleon's principles, plebiscites were ordered. The people voted, almost unanimously, for joining France.

So Napoleon had taken the decisive step toward the liberation of Italy, scored hollow but resounding victories, avoided a general war, won two provinces. And again he had achieved the rarest success: a settlement that left no bitterness. At Villafranca, the two emperors had met as friends, and friends they remained until the end of the regime. The Austrian Ambassador, Prince Richard Metternich, and especially his wife, Princess Pauline, were great favorites in Parisian society.

The end of the war was marked by rejoicings such as France had not seen for fifty years, and was not to know again until 1918. On the 14th of August 1859, the veterans of the Italian campaign marched in triumph down the boulevards, the Emperor at their head. When they reached the Place Vendôme, Napoleon saluted the Empress with his sword, took his little son on his saddle, and watched the tattered regiments as they passed in review. Most wildly acclaimed were the Zouaves, who, with their Algerian uniforms, their dash, their cool tenacity, had become heroes of legend. For another seven or eight years prosperity was to grow even more dazzling; prestige, on the surface, would remain unimpaired; but this was the summit of the reign. Napoleon III wanted to mark his triumph by an act of reconciliation. The next day, August 15, the national holiday under the Empire, all exiles were amnestied without conditions; most of them returned. The military establishment was reduced: at last, "the Empire was to mean: *Peace.*"

CHAPTER SIX

THE GLITTER AND THE GOLD
1852–1870

AGAINST the main front of the Paris Opéra stands Car-
peaux's wonderful group *The Dance*: a ring of laugh-
ing bacchants, drunk with music and motion, and in the
center the haunting figure of a Genius, tense, mephis-
tophelian, yet with the wistfulness of higher things.
When the statuary was unveiled, a puritan hurled an
ink bottle at one of the whirling nymphs. It was the
same gesture as Martin Luther's three and a half centuries before; in both cases there was no appreciable result: the devil thrives on ink.

Charles Garnier's Opéra is often considered as the
typical monument of the Gaudy Empire, and Car-
peaux's group as the aptest symbol of the period and of
the regime. To the dispassionate art critic, the building
seems particularly functional: an Opéra is not a Quaker
meeting house, and there should be richness and gaiety
about a temple of luxurious pleasure. At any rate, Garnier's masterpiece has been pastiched in every clime,
from exuberant São Paulo and Rio de Janeiro to Cal-
vin's holy city, Geneva. The patina of age has merci-
fully toned down the dazzling whiteness of the stone,
softened the vivid polychromy of the marbles, mellowed
the aggressive splendor of the gildings. The proverb
that the Opéra best illustrates might well be: "All is not
tinsel that glitters."

It would of course be unfair to consider the Opéra
as the master key to the Second Empire. Many churches

were built at that time, some of them not without taste. Napoleon III had given orders that work on the Opéra should be kept behind the reconstruction of the Hôtel-Dieu, the great general hospital on the island of the City. Baltard's central market, Les Halles, remains a monument of spare and elegant adequacy, and it too was imitated throughout the world. But a caricature, exaggerating a single feature, may be cruelly true. Cyrano de Bergerac was not a nose with a human being appended; still, he was afflicted with a memorable nose. The Empire was by no means all garishness; but the garishness was undeniable.

Prosperity was the characteristic of the Second Empire, as glory had been of the First. That prosperity was different from the drab and cautious well-being which was the goal of the Constitutional Monarchy. It was sudden, and on an unprecedented scale. It seemed even more miraculous after the years of turmoil and uneasiness of the Second Republic. This made it assertive and blatant. The profiteers did not quite believe in their good fortune, and they had to give themselves tangible proofs of its reality. England was well ahead of France in the industrial and financial transformation that marked the third quarter of the century, and there was at least as much conspicuous waste north as south of the Channel: virtuous as were the Royal Pair, the Albert Memorial can hardly be called a model of chaste design. But in Britain there were enough families of ancient wealth and breeding to temper the crudity of the new rich. That element was lacking in French society. The old nobility, staunch in their Legitimist faith, had gone into social mourning. Their châteaux had become fortresses again, in which they defied the vulgarity of modern progress.

Their quarter in Paris, the faubourg Saint-Germain, turned its back on Parisian life. To the casual visitor it offered an array of dingy silent streets: only the initiated could be aware of the old-world gardens and of the tasteful salons behind the flaking gray walls. The substantial bourgeoisie—long lines of landowners and magistrates—deprecated the fever and the tumult of the new age. Politically, the conservative classes voted for Napoleon III—with misgivings. Socially, they went into a self-imposed exile. Their places could be filled only by parvenus. In the proclamation announcing his marriage, Napoleon III defiantly called himself a parvenu Emperor.

He wanted a court. Not out of sheer vanity, but in order to prove that France had triumphantly emerged from the stodginess of the Louis-Philippe era and to demonstrate that the old aristocracy was not indispensable, even as an ornament. The court was to set the social tone. Its luxury was to be a national advertisement and a national asset. On a hint from Persigny, the Emperor was given a fabulous civil list, five million dollars a year, twice as much as he had expected. Out of this vast sum he could afford lavish personal charities. He secretly pensioned, for example, the poet Leconte de Lisle, who was a political enemy. He took care of the national palaces: the Louvre and the Tuileries were completed at last, and Viollet-le-Duc was given perhaps too free a rein in the restoration of ancient edifices. But Napoleon had a handsome balance to play with, and he spent it conscientiously. At the Tuileries, at Saint-Cloud, at Compiègne, at Fontainebleau, he entertained on a magnificent scale. Gone were those court functions to which the thrifty haberdashers of the rue du Sentier would repair in an omnibus. Court dress and uniforms were now *de rigueur*. For the stag hunts at Fontaine-bleau, eighteenth-century costumes were revived.

The court of the first Napoleon too had been re-splendent; but it was stiff, frigid, and intensely boring. The autocrat, although he could produce at will a most charming smile, remained the martinet; he would pass in review the ladies of his court with the glare, the frown, and the imperial brevity of a top sergeant. Under Napoleon III, court life was elaborately dignified: that means that it could be tedious at times. The "orgies of the Tuileries" may be dismissed as a mere phrase, not even a myth. Yet between the official world and the world of pleasure, there were no impassable barriers and no radical difference in tone. The Empress was virtuous, and far less flighty than her heroine Marie Antoinette: there was not even a Fersen in her life. But the Emperor had acquired her as "the crown's most precious jewel." He wanted her to assume the leadership of fashion, and we know that she required very little urging. In these triumphs, however, she was barely keeping ahead of those ladies fair and frail who were such a feature of imperial Paris, Cora Pearl, Anna Deslions, Juliette Ba-rucci, La Païva, a quaint fauna of "lionesses, does, and cranes" ("*lionnes, biches et grues*"). Vaudeville artists like Theresa performed even in aristocratic homes and mingled freely with the guests. In fancy-dress balls, the social strata were willfully fused. The Empress was ever on the watch for any alluring mask who might attract the attention of her susceptible consort.

In this respect the imperial circle and the most ques-tionable aspects of *la vie parisienne* became inseparable in the public mind. The very highest, the Emperor him-

self, Morny, Prince Napoleon, were notorious for their
freedom from bourgeois prejudices. Second Empire society was not *French* in character: it was *Gallic*, it was
Frenchy; which means that it was cosmopolitan, even
more cosmopolitan than the Paris of the Pompadour
era. Napoleon III, it will be remembered, could be
described as a one-man United Nations. The Empress
had roamed the whole of Europe. Princess Mathilde,
Prince Napoleon, were half Württemberg; she wedded
a Russian prince, he an Italian princess. The Countess
de Morny was a Russian. Walewski was a Pole, his
wife a Florentine. With a slight twist, the old gibe
would serve: "There is but one Frenchman in the
whole lot, Persigny; and he is mad." If we were to
pick out the most nearly perfect representatives of imperial Paris, our choice would go to Princess Pauline
Metternich, the Austrian Ambassadress, and to Jacques
Offenbach, the composer of scandalously tuneful oper-
ettas. She came from Vienna, he from Cologne.

Here we must guard against a confusion hoary with
age—three centuries at least—and apparently indestructible. The word *libertin* in French first meant a
freethinker, and then, as if by a natural consequence, a
man of dissolute life. It might be thought that the moral
laxity of the Second Empire was linked with the progress
of unbelief. This is far from the truth. In the main,
Bonapartism and clericalism were close allies. Priests
were as welcome at the Tuileries as generals. The Emperor, in his unaccountable way, was actually pious.
When he went incognito through Paris, inspecting the
public works in which he was so passionately interested,
he would stop at a church and, unnoticed except by his
confidential attendant, kneel in prayer. Morny had the

proper attitude of the *grand seigneur* and the profiteer: never wrestle with religious problems, for fear of having to take them seriously. Prince Napoleon alone was, ostensibly, both a scoffer and a rake: but he was not held up as a pattern to the imperial world. On the other hand, the skeptics so virulently denounced by the Catholic journalist Louis Veuillot were actually men of irreproachable integrity, like Taine and Renan, or even "secular saints" like the Positivist Littré.

There is one respect in which the Second Empire stood for "free thought" in every sense of that elastic term. For the first eight years at least, it was a police state, pitiless to agitators, not tender even to honest critics: it was hardly safe to attack the Emperor, except under the pseudonyms of Soulouque and Tiberius. But even at its worst it did not attempt to stifle convictions or crush ideas. This was not owing purely to the secret gentleness of the Emperor: the regime itself was too much of a hybrid, the society over which it ruled was too hopelessly divided, for an orthodoxy to be strictly imposed. The statutes and the *mores* of a country may tell different stories. According to the letter of the law, no country at that time was freer than England. But, as Hilaire Belloc remarked, there existed in Victorian society "a sort of cohesive public spirit [which] glued and immobilized all individual expression. One could float imprisoned as in a stream of thick substance, one could not swim against it." The public spirit of the Second Empire was not cohesive: that is why it was so intensely alive. P. J. Proudhon, who had said: "Property is theft" and "God is evil," could write undisturbed to the end, and remain on friendly terms with the first prince of the blood. Catholics and Protestants of all shades, hu-

manitarians, freethinkers, Voltairian rationalists, Saint-
Simonians, Positivists, mystics, devil-worshippers, scientists, anarchists, socialists, believers in art for art's sake,
all could fearlessly voyage to the end of their thought.
The important point is not that, in one egregious year,
both Flaubert and Baudelaire were haled before a court
of justice—the one to be acquitted, the other sentenced
to an insignificant fine; it is that *Madame Bovary* and
The Flowers of Evil could be written. On a solemn
occasion Napoleon III said, with the hand on the hilt
of his sword: "Material order is my responsibility," and
critics shook their doleful heads: "Ah! a purely materialistic regime!" No: a regime aware that certain
things are Cæsar's, and first of all order in the streets;
and that other things pertain to the spirit.

"We must admit," Taine wrote in his *Travel Notes*
(1863–5), "that there is in this country a sudden expansion of public prosperity, similar to the upsurge that
marked the Renaissance or the times of Colbert. This
year, two thousand miles of railroads were built. The
Emperor understands France and his century better than
any of his predecessors." Taine was no blind supporter
of the regime; the verdict was unanimous; the opposition
could only spurn material progress, not deny its reality.
A whole generation after Sedan, when I was a school-
boy, the "good times" of the Empire survived in the
popular mind as a golden memory.

Like all legends, this is not "the humble truth" of the
naturalists, but an epic amplification. All was not for the
best in that glittering paradise. The masses, urban and
rural, lived under conditions that the hard-pinched
Fourth Republic would not tolerate. The Empire had

to face constant difficulties not of its own making. In the early years, floods, crop failures, a near-famine, an epidemic of cholera, darkened the economic scene; for the first time in the century, the years 1854 and 1855 were marked by a deficit of births. Then there was a disease of the silkworm; and at that time France was producing much of the raw material woven in the capital of that trade, Lyon. The oïdium first, and a transatlantic blight, the phylloxera, attacked the vines, an ancient source of wealth. The American Civil War played havoc with the cotton interests. The three great wars, the Crimea, Italy, Mexico, drained resources without compensation. Yet there was steady progress in the teeth of these stubborn obstacles.

Some countries have been noted for their fantastic luxury for the privileged and hopeless destitution among the masses: such was the case with the India of the rajahs, and with colonial Mexico. Not so with the France of Napoleon III. There was splendor, some of it meretricious; there was squalor, some of it heart-rending; but there was no abyss between the many and the few. The great majority were neither paupers nor spendthrifts, but hard-working common men. The lot of the most modest was improving, and the road to wealth was open to the ambitious. Most of all, there was a sense of expansion, of illimitable hope, that was truly exhilarating. The Empire was a state of mind rather than an array of statistics. That state of mind should be familiar to us: it has been ours from the very beginning, and has scarcely suffered an eclipse. It faded from France after Sedan, and it has never been fully recovered.

The economic brilliancy of the Second Empire was not a delusive flash, like the Mississippi Bubble under

the Regency, Calonne's hectic flare of wild spending on
the eve of the Revolution, or the phosphorescence of the
Thermidorian reaction and the early Directoire. Because
it spread deep, that prosperity proved enduring. It outlasted the eighteen years of the reign. The catastrophes
of 1870–1—the collapse of the imperial armies, the
reckless and hopeless efforts of Gambetta's National Defense, the Commune, the five billion francs exacted by
Prussia—failed to dissipate the solid wealth of the country. Bismarck had expected that France would be bled
white for a generation: within two years the unprecedented indemnity was paid off. The reserves that made
the settlement easy had not been created by Adolphe
Thiers, who got credit for the operation; they had been
accumulated under Napoleon III.

It may be contended that Napoleon III simply happened to reach power at the right moment. It was not
he who had started the financial revolution, the creation
of modern capitalism: it had been under way in Holland and England since the seventeenth century, well
ahead of the machine age. Here we find once more the
two conceptions of history confronting each other, the
personal and the collective. I have already expressed my
conviction that, in a certain perspective, the course of
human events dwarfs all individual endeavor: the evolution of Europe could be traced without Luther, Cal-
vin, or Rousseau; without Louis XIV, Frederick the
Great, or Napoleon I; without Newton, Kant, Hegel,
Darwin; without Adam Smith or Karl Marx. A great
name is invariably a symbol rather than a cause. But if
we deal in decades rather than æons, personalities make
a difference. Within the vast cycles of obscure anony-
mous efforts, the foresight and determination of actual

leaders, or their obstinacy and frivolous ignorance, can be of vital importance. There were railroads in France from the early days of Louis-Philippe, and inventors like Marc Séguin had made most valuable contributions to their development. But Adolphe Thiers, eminently practical, neither dull nor flippant, the incarnation of sound common sense, could only sneer at those elaborate "toys"; Lamartine, the poet, saw their future. In many respects Napoleon III stood far closer to Lamartine than to Adolphe Thiers; both had a largeness of heart and vision which made them scorn *petit bourgeois* timidity. It is not a matter of indifference that France before 1848 and after 1870 was almost invariably governed, not by the élite and not by the masses, but by the congeners of Thiers, the lower middle class.

If a statesman professes to serve at the same time two antagonistic tendencies, he is accused either of confusion or of duplicity: as if in mechanics a component of forces were not an elementary conception. Men who adopt what they think is a merciful attitude toward Napoleon III praise the generosity of his "dreams" and deplore their vagueness. Vagueness? The record of his reign gives a totally different impression. There is nothing vague about Napoleon III's policies; we have to deal neither with a utopian nor with a doctrinaire, but with a realist who had a purpose and a method. The purpose was the service of the whole people: he was a democrat of the Cæsarian type—and therefore a socialist; it is not the purpose of a government to foster private interests, but to harmonize those interests for the general good. The state is a great co-operative; its first duty, in the words of Saint-Simon, is to promote the material and moral welfare of the most numerous and poorest elements. The first condition of progress, let this never be forgotten for a moment, is order; but in an atmosphere of calm and confidence, all classes could contribute to the prosperity of the *common wealth*. This idea had been expressed by Queen Hortense in her *Memoirs* with surprising clarity, and had been ascribed by her to Napoleon I. From that ideal, with a gentle obstinacy that puzzled theorists and fanatics, Napoleon III never swerved.

Oddly, the *social* character of Napoleon's rule was implicit in the title that the conservatives had bestowed upon him: if he had "saved Society," it must have been for Society's own good, not for the benefit of a few. In a more literal sense, he was an avowed socialist. His little book, hardly more than a pamphlet, *On the Extinction of Pauperism*, was a rudimentary but practical statement of his principles. On the strength of it he was hailed by Louis Blanc and George Sand as one of their company. His scheme—the working of unused land by a reserve army of labor, self-governing, but directed by the State—implied the central idea of 1848: the right to a job. The Emperor redeemed the pledge of the publicist. He insisted that public works should be directly authorized by himself, and as soon as he was in full power, in 1852, he started a program of public works in the spirit of his proposals of 1844. He turned Louis Blanc's "National Workshops," so woefully, so willfully sabotaged in 1848, into successful realities. In Sologne, in the Dombes, he drained marshes; in the Landes, he carried out a long-neglected plan, and the shifting sand dunes were fixed by plantations of pines. There is hardly any rural district in which some modest, useful work was not done. At the summit of these ubi-

quitous activities we find the great spectacular enterprises, railroads, canals, ports, city improvements, and,
most sensational of all, the reconstruction of Paris. Such
a policy is the stock-in-trade of all dictators—Mussolini, Hitler, Huey Long—and it is one of the reasons
why, in spite of their obvious perils, dictatorships have
such an appeal: *things get done*. It was not wrong of
Napoleon III—or Mussolini—to drain marshes. Let
party politicians demonstrate that they have the same
large views and the same efficiency as the dictators, and
liberty will be considerably safer.

Napoleon III was the elect of small farmers, and he
did his best for them. But his heart was not in the land:
like his contemporary Baudelaire, "he could not wax
lyrical about vegetables." He looked into the future, and
he could see that in France the prospects of agriculture
were limited: the land had been cultivated for centuries, and modern methods would only reduce the need
for human labor. The dream of Marshal Pétain, a
France predominantly rural, attached to an economy of
small peasant proprietors, would have admirably served
the purposes of Hitler, for its destiny would have been
irremediable decadence. Napoleon III's chief interest
was industry.

That interest was not intellectual merely, but intimate. Napoleon III never was fully convincing as a
soldier; perhaps even less as a prince of the Renaissance,
a patron of the arts; and he could not, like David Lloyd
George, don the corduroys of the country squire and
find pride and joy in raising prize-winning hogs. His
very hobbies were mechanical: he was compared with
the gentle-eyed White Knight of Lewis Carroll, surrounded with gadgets "all of his own invention." In his

last days, he was working on an economical stove for
the poor. There was in him a Jules Verne or, more obviously, an H. G. Wells: a romanticist whose dreams
were of the future, not of the past, and translated themselves into terms of engineering. Even when he dabbled
in archæology, it was Cæsar's war machines that fas-
cinated him.

For at least half a millennium, France had been great
in the arts and crafts: the eighteenth century marked the
apex of that exquisite tradition. The good artisan, who
loves his trade and his tools, who creates a personal piece
of work for a personal and competent customer, is still
with us; and the spirit that made him great in his limited
field may be transferred to industrial design. But we
must admit that the bulk of our goods has to be machine-
made; and the machine demands new methods and a
new ideology. This is not always realized, even by
responsible leaders: the cultural lag is not an empty
phrase. In England, businessmen proudly assume feudal
titles, or pose as gentlemen farmers. In America, great
engineers cling to the economy of *The Village Black-
smith*. Napoleon III, as Taine put it, understood his
century; his handicaps were those of the forerunner, not
of the fossil. He realized quite simply that modern industry is, by its very nature, collectivistic. The co-
operation of the many is needed to supply the wants of
the many. Communism is conceivable without machine
production: the religious orders prove the point. But it
is impossible to imagine an industrial age founded on
sheer individualism.

Hardly more than a century ago, sturdy Auvergnats
brought water up to Parisian apartments for a few cents
a pail, a model of free enterprise and rugged individual-

ism. When water was piped from central reservoirs, the individual carrier was doomed. The new service had to be collectivistic, whether managed by a private company, by a semi-public authority, or by the city itself. It is the change in technique that killed the old-fashioned free competition. The revolution was not in the laws or in the minds: it was in the pipes.

Napoleon III, as defender and promoter of the common interest, accepted this indispensable collectivism of modern life. But he did not commit himself to any exclusive doctrine. He encouraged and subsidized the co-operative system. But the customers failed to respond: even in England, co-operative societies have remained a secondary factor. He was not afraid of state capitalism, or direct management by the government. Since officials could be entrusted with such "big business" as the armed forces, the postal service, great public works, there was no reason why they could not as well run a mine or a railroad. But he accepted also, as a genuine form of collectivism, the corporation, which, if it performed a public service, should be authorized and supervised by the State in the interests of the community. From the capitalistic point of view, nothing could be more orthodox than the corporation. Yet it marks a definite deviation from strict private property, *jus utendi et abutendi*, "I can do what I please with my own." It is a property that is shared, and that entails social responsibilities.

Napoleon III's pragmatic attitude is well illustrated by his railroad policy. The fiction that railroads could be left entirely to private initiative and unlimited competition resulted in sluggish construction and feverish speculation, for it is only on paper that any one can start a railroad. Even in modern America, railroads are treated as public services. The managing companies cannot open or close a line or alter a tariff without the consent of some government agency. In cases of emergency—war or threat of strike—they are taken over by the State. Under Napoleon III, innumerable rival lines were consolidated into six regional systems, with a ninety-nine-year franchise, a minimum dividend guaranteed by the State, and definite responsibilities to the State. From these six semi-public corporations, the transition was easy to a "National Company," still capitalistic in form. As in the case of the water supply, it was the change in technique, the creation of the railroads themselves, that brought about the collectivistic revolution; the method of financial administration was a secondary matter.

P. J. Proudhon, a critical and very intelligent observer, described this policy as "a new feudalism." He meant it as a term of reproach: feudalism had lost its vitality even before the close of the Middle Ages, and its fossilized remains had to be swept away by the Revolution. But in theory the system (in so far as it ever was a system) was superior to the anarchic conception of absolute individual ownership. In feudal doctrine, no one possessed anything outright. Authority and property were closely bound together; both were merely delegated; they conferred privileges, but they entailed obligations. A *concessionnaire* is indeed a vassal, and he may have sub-vassals in his turn. He swears fealty to his suzerain; that is to say that he promises to observe the terms of his franchise. The profit motive is not ignored, but it is subordinated to the common good, of which the sover-

eign, whatever his title may be, stands as the symbol
and supreme guardian.

Large-scale and long-range enterprise, characteristic
of the Second Empire and of the modern world as a
whole, demands planning. This, in the France of one
hundred years ago, required in its turn a revolution in
finance, forward-looking credit emphasized instead of
mere day-by-day saving. For ages, the ideal of the peasant and of the *petit bourgeois* had been to spend a little
less than he earned; with the pennies thus hoarded in
the traditional "woolen stocking," he could buy another
field, another house, another government bond. Thrift
was the only recognized key to wealth. Under all systems, saving remains the indispensable basis; and we
do not deny the admirable qualities of hard work and
self-denial which went with the old French state of
mind. But as a result, investors were struck with con-
genital timidity: their *pauvres petits quatre sous*, their
pennies so painfully saved, the fruit of such long toil and
constant privation, could not be risked in distant ven-
turesome investments. Credit was gambling, and gambling was sin. John Law, early in the eighteenth century, had revealed the magic of credit; but in the eyes
of the safe and sane, his Icarus fall was a well-deserved
lesson.

There was very little of the French bourgeois about
Napoleon III: he was a cosmopolitan adventurer. I
have called him a gambler for the highest stakes; he had
lost two fortunes on his way to power. But he was not
a mere gambler, and his reign was not a fabulous Monte
Carlo. He was an industrialist, not a financier; a builder,
not a profiteer. "Enterprise" means pioneering, opening

new paths, and some of these may lead to disaster: Lesseps won against the sands of Suez, but lost against the
mosquitoes of Panama. Among the many daring ventures
in which France engaged under the Second Empire,
some went bankrupt. But on the whole, considered as
a great economic campaign, the regime was a success.
After the disasters of 1870–1—diplomatic, military,
political—the State, the great cities, the banks, private
business, were all in good financial health.

Credit is another word for speculation; and speculation, when isolated from production, means the enrich-
ment of the profiteer. The important point is that under
the Second Empire production remained the essential
element, speculation a mere gilded fringe; whereas at
the time of John Law the economic basis of his dizzy
"System" had been perilously slender. No doubt the
profiteer was a conspicuous element in Second Empire
life. The most daring, the most ruthless, the most urbane
of them all was Morny, half-brother of the Emperor,
co-founder of the regime, and one of its most brilliant
ornaments. A whisper: "Morny is in it," sufficed to
bring forth an approving nod: "Then it must be a good
thing." But even Morny was more than the king of
gamblers: he had sound business sense. The only great
venture of his that ended disastrously (not for himself,
but for France) was his getting an interest in the Jecker
Bonds: a preposterous debt that a Swiss banker was attempting to collect from Mexico.

It happened that Haussmann, prefect of the Seine,
repeatedly bought property that soon afterwards was
condemned for the opening of a new thoroughfare. But
although the opposition jeered at "Haussmann's Fantastic Accounts" (a punning allusion to Hoffmann's *Fan-*

tastic Tales), he was first of all a most efficient public servant. The existence of the profiteer under Napoleon III cannot be denied. The type belongs to the ages; oddly enough, it had been most vividly described by Balzac, who died in 1850, and by Lesage, whose *Turcaret* was performed in 1709. Literature is prophecy as well as chronicle. But the Second Empire was not run by and for the profiteers.

With his concern for the common good, Napoleon III attempted to "nationalize" credit. Hitherto, half a dozen great bankers had held the whole market in fee: the French branch of the Rothschilds served as the symbol of that oligarchy. Now state and municipal bonds were offered directly to the masses: thus there could be a state capitalism on the grandest scale, without a special class of capitalists. The great loans of the Empire were financial plebiscites: direct expressions of popular confidence. They were invariably oversubscribed: the peasant supported the regime not merely with his vote, but with his woolen stocking. Thus were reconciled and profitably associated the national virtue of thrift and the Napoleonic—or American—quality of daring.

Most typical of the Empire were credit institutions of a semi-public nature. The charter of the Bank of France was renewed; its association with the State was made closer; and branches were opened in every department. The Crédit Foncier (1852) was a national building loan association, lending on mortgages to departments, cities, and private owners. The Crédit Mobilier (1852) financed railroads, ports, public utilities, navigation companies. The Crédit Industriel was created in 1859, the Crédit Lyonnais in 1863, the Société Générale pour Favoriser le Développement du Commerce et de l'In-

dustrie en France in 1864: the cumbrous name might
serve as a subtitle for the Empire itself. All but one of
these survived into our own days. They were the financial armature of the Third Republic; and the Fourth,
carrying out the intentions of Napoleon III, made them
in fact organs of the State. They have been honestly,
efficiently, and successfully managed. Only the Crédit
Mobilier, which, under the Pereire brothers, played a
great part in the activities of the reign, became a victim
to excessive daring and the jealousy of its rivals: in 1867
bankruptcy could be averted only through a drastic reorganization that involved heavy losses to the general
public.

The most lasting, the most impressive monument of
the Second Empire was the reconstruction of the cities.
This was not limited to Paris: Marseille, in particular,
owes more to the eighteen years of Napoleon III than
to the preceding twenty-five hundred. The transformation of Paris, naturally, stands apart on account of its
magnitude and of its magnificence.

In the public mind the work is usually connected
with the name of Baron Haussmann. For all the flaws of
his temper and of his taste, the great prefect of the Seine
was no doubt an admirable servant of the State. But he
was an instrument: Napoleon III had conceived the
plan himself. On the wall of his study he had a large
map of Paris with the proposed improvements drawn
with his own hands, in blue, red, yellow, and green,
according to their urgency. He found his first prefect,
Berger, too timid; so, in the early months of the Empire,
he cast about for a man of greater daring and energy.
He selected Haussmann, who had shown great vigor
in the administration of Bordeaux.

Haussmann firmly believed in a strong executive. He was in full harmony with his sovereign and enjoyed his confidence: in his department he had practically *carte blanche*. There was no elected municipal council to play ward politics and obstruct far-seeing measures: only an appointed commission, as still is the case with Washington, D.C. When the Empire veered toward liberalism, Haussmann was exposed to fierce attacks; when, in 1870, the regime turned into a constitutional monarchy, Haussmann resigned.

To rebuild a great historic capital is a gigantic task; like all great enterprises, it was not the working out of a single idea. All the explanations that have been offered are right, provided not one of them is considered as exclusive and self-sufficient. The most obvious is the strategic interpretation: Napoleon III, guardian of material order, wanted to prevent the recurrence of those insurrections which in 1827, 1830, 1832, 1834, 1839, four times in 1848, in 1849, in 1851, had shaken or destroyed the national government. Wide, straight avenues surrounded or slashed through the old workingmen's districts. They could be swept by cavalry charges or raked by artillery fire. For twenty years there was no menacing disorder in the streets. Ironically, these elaborate preparations proved a Maginot Line: the Empire fell without a single shot. Most of the improvements, however, cannot be explained on that score. Dangerous areas were still untouched by 1870; and impressive works had been carried out in the west, where no insurrection was to be feared.

Autocratic governments revel in showy public works: they are advertisements on a gigantic scale. "The glory is remembered when the cost is forgotten." The com-

pletion of the Louvre might fall into that category, but
it simply fulfilled at last the dream of two centuries and
more. The Opéra is obviously a case in point: it was a
jeweled crown on the brow of the city, and, like most
crowns, a costly bauble. But the greater part of the work
done in Paris was not intended to be spectacular. If the
Auteuil Viaduct, for instance, has a truly Roman dignity, it was none the less functional at the time. The
greatest municipal achievement of the Second Empire
was the work of Belgrand. The sewer system of old
Paris, so admirably described in *Les Misérables,* was
sheer chaos, and the water supply was inadequate. Belgrand created both services on truly modern lines and
on the proper scale. Had the regime lasted, Belgrand
might have carried out his plan for a ship channel from
Paris to the sea.

No doubt the great public works throughout France,
and particularly those in Paris, were intended as an in-
surance against unemployment. They were in line with
Napoleon's own little book: *On the Extinction of
Pauperism.* They were meant also to "prime the pump."
The proverb ran: "When the building trades thrive,
everything thrives." But the whole scheme was not primarily devised to serve some other purpose. The most
direct explanation is the most adequate: Napoleon
wanted these improvements because he believed them to
be improvements. They were simply part of his Saint-
Simonian program: the common welfare.

He was well acquainted with the West End of London; he had admired the wide streets, the dignified fa-
çades, the many leafy squares; and he was not satisfied
with picturesque squalor. He wished to reconstruct
Paris, as he wished to reconstruct Europe, because he

was persuaded that man-made ills could be cured by human foresight and energy. He stood, not for unconscious haphazard growth, the alibi of the lazy-minded, but for determination and planning.

New districts, new cities, had been designed before: Versailles, St. Petersburg, Washington. Paris offered an infinitely more delicate problem: to recast an ancient metropolis, heavy with the riches and the grime of age, without destroying its spirit and its charm. From the practical point of view, the work was brilliantly successful. Although the plans of Napoleon and Haussmann slowed down almost to a standstill after Sedan, they remained adequate for half a century. The actual formula of Haussmann is now antiquated; but the spirit of Haussmann—of Napoleon III—would be needed if we were boldly to grapple with our present problems.

From the æsthetic point of view, the work is not free from blemishes. Some delightful aspects of old Paris were unnecessarily sacrificed. Many of the new buildings, private and public, were manifestly mediocre. It is fashionable to deplore the "devastations" wrought by the Emperor and his prefect. Yet in the eyes neither of foreign visitors nor of the Parisians themselves has the city lost its magic appeal. It is easy to grow sentimental about the rue de la Huchette, a slum forgotten within a stone's throw of Notre-Dame, but we remain thankful that Paris is not a maze of malodorous lanes. What strikes us on the contrary about the work of Napoleon III, in all domains, is that, although so bold, it was at the same time profoundly conservative. No radicalism *à la* Le Corbusier, who would raze the whole of central Paris and erect on the site a stiff array of cruciform skyscrapers. In scale, spirit, and style the new Paris was

not different from the old. The best features of the royal
tradition were not discarded or ignored, but extended.
The boulevard Malesherbes resembled the boulevard
des Capucines; the Pont de l'Alma, a robust and elegant
stone bridge, was in harmony with the Pont de la Con-
corde.

Here we have to face a puzzling situation. Napoleon III kept Paris employed, made it healthier, more
prosperous, more brilliant; yet from first to last, Paris
on the whole remained hostile to the regime. We can
understand this attitude on the part of the "liberal"
bourgeoisie: although its prosperity had increased, the
class as such had lost something of its prestige. Above
all, it had been robbed of its favorite pastimes, parliamentary eloquence and the political game. But, except
for a brief period during the Italian campaign, the Parisian masses were inflexibly anti-Bonapartist. For twenty
years France offered the paradox of a leader endorsed by
those who understood him least, the rural population,
and rejected by those whom he was most eager to benefit, industrial labor.

The cause of this apparent absurdity is that, a century ago, Paris thought in political, not in economic or
social terms. In 1863 Paris gave 400 votes to labor
candidates, 153,000 to the bourgeois opposition, led
by the royalist Thiers, hater of "the vile multitude."
The workers were democrats rather than socialists; it
might even be said that they were republicans rather
than democrats, for they never accepted the peasants as
their equals, and the tremendous majorities piled up by
Napoleon III impressed them not at all: rural votes are
not valid votes. All they chose to remember was that

Napoleon had destroyed a parliamentary republic, although that republic was anti-democratic at the time. To govern without the assent of Paris, in their eyes, was a crime of *lèse-majesté* against the spirit. The Commune was the last flare of that mystic belief in the messianic character of Paris; a romantic myth, preached by Victor Hugo and even by Alfred de Vigny, it now reposes in the dim Pantheon of dead gods. At any rate, Paris could neither be bribed by imperial prosperity, seduced by imperial splendor, nor coerced by the imperial police. This stubborn resistance for the sake of an ideal may not have been very wise. At any rate, it could not be called ignoble.

CHAPTER SEVEN

THE SULTRY YEARS
1860–1867

WE have left Napoleon III, on the 14th and 15th of August 1859, at the pinnacle of his glory. He had returned victorious from a brief and popular campaign, which he had commanded in person. He had magnanimously granted an amnesty to his political enemies. To be sure, there were, even then, discordant voices prophesying his decline and fall. Victor Hugo did not waver for a moment in his inexorable hatred. We know the end of the story, and we may delude ourselves into the belief that Sedan was inevitable, as it was not avoided. *Whatever is, is right*: this kind of fatalism, although endorsed by Alexander Pope and Ella Wheeler Wilcox, is repugnant to the Western mind. There are ineluctable laws in nature: but within these laws, blind chance and the will of men, not mechanical determinism alone, shape the course of human events. The career of Napoleon III is a drama because at every step several possibilities were open. It is idle to speculate on what might have been; but if we want to recapture the spirit of a hundred years ago, we must never forget that even the most astute among the contemporaries could not know for certain what was to happen next. The death of an individual is an accident: Billault and Morny need not have died so soon; another Orsini might have taken a better aim.

A regime with a sensational beginning must lose something of its magic as soon as the first surprise is over.

After a few years conservative France took material order and prosperity for granted. True, with us, the memory of the Great Depression and the fair promises of the
New Deal soon faded away. But the Second Empire
was not static; it did not live on the prestige of a single
moment; it was capable of change and growth. The
prosperity of the age never became humdrum: the government was constantly seeking new lines of development. It might be said that the Napoleonic regime was
founded on two ideas, Order and Progress, so antagonistic that the attempt to reconcile them was bound to fail.
But such a contradiction is inherent in every government: it might better be met by constant adjustment
than by a series of jolts. The difficulties of the 1860's
were not radically different from those of the '50's. Had
Napoleon III remained equal to himself, he would have
been equal to the problems of the second decade.

The Second Empire was a personal regime, and its
deterioration was that of its ruler. In essentials Napoleon III did not change: at fifty and sixty he was gently
stubborn as he had been in his youth, profoundly kind,
reticent, with an unswerving faith in his destiny, yet
with an odd streak of humility. The more dangerous
aspects of his character—at times the most attractive—
survived also: he was secretive, a utopian, an adventurer, a conspirator to the end. He had not grown stale;
but he had turned weak.

The first cause of this weakness was physiological.
For most men, the fifties are still the prime of life. But
Napoleon aged beyond his years. He had recovered
from the anemia induced by his years of imprisonment,
and his many minor ailments were mere annoyances.
But soon after 1860 he suffered increasingly from a

stone in the bladder. He bore his suffering stoically: in the last campaign, he remained for hours in the saddle when every moment was torture. But the pain had a numbing effect. Even intermittent, even dulled by seda tives, that pain would sap the magnificent self-assurance indispensable to a leader. Napoleon III had hours and days of surcease, and brief revivals of the old quiet energy. His mind was not clouded; his good will was unimpaired; but his will power was damaged. The Na poleon of 1852 could make full use of a Rouher: he would not have allowed, out of sheer lassitude, such a coarse instrument to become a Vice-Emperor.

His conduct was affected by his devotion to his only child, the none too robust little Prince Imperial. All hopes of a long and strenuous career for himself had to be abandoned: his one thought was to transmit, at the earliest possible moment, a steady throne to his heir. The dynastic principle, which he had rejected in his program matic book *Napoleonic Ideas*, became his Nemesis. It blurred his political sense. It made him more conservative at a time when his sensitive intelligence was telling him that the way out was forward. It made him less daring, but, alas, not invariably more prudent. Had the throne been elective, he could have retired as soon as he dis covered that infirmities were sapping his vigor. But he could not abdicate: he knew that the Empress, as regent, would have been capricious and unpopular. He had to wait until his son could be declared of age, in 1874. As late as midsummer 1870 this did not seem an unreason able hope.

This ardent love for their son was the one great bond between the Emperor and the Empress. When the prince was concerned, both parents were "legitimists," an absurd attitude in a sovereign who claimed to rule, not by the right of birth, but "by the will of the people." But this parental affection was not the only cause of Eugénie's increasing influence. Napoleon had loved her passionately; he still loved her deeply. He was all the more reluctant to oppose her wishes, as he was conscious of his repeated marital transgressions. He made up to the Empress for his manifold sins against the wife. Not for the country's good. Persigny, who had conjugal troubles of his own, and whose fanatical devotion to the Bonapartist cause excused the roughest candor, could tell his sovereign, as man to man: "Nos femmes nous coûtent cher" ("Our wives are a heavy burden"). And we surmise that Napoleon took silent refuge behind his impenetrable stare.

Eugénie had elected Marie Antoinette as her heroine and pattern. She too was, all too eagerly, the refulgent queen of fashion. She too came to despise in her heart her gentle consort: with far less justification, for Napoleon III was not a Louis XVI. She grew impatient when he silently attempted to unravel a political problem. She had spirit, like a thoroughbred; but spirit is not a safe substitute for mind. In public affairs, she believed in a haughty, truculent attitude, which she mistook for firmness and energy; and she used the same forcible methods in private life. The Tuileries resounded at times with her angry voice—a courtier or a flunky behind every door. She threatened, and caused, scandal: she rushed away in a rage, once as far as Scotland in the wrong season, once to Schwalbach near Wiesbaden. Napoleon could face physical danger, without bravado but with stolid courage; he found it harder to face conjugal scenes.

The Empress was regent three times: during the
Italian campaign, during Napoleon's triumphal visit to
Algeria (1865), and during the Franco-Prussian War.
This official status justified her in bursting in upon cabinet meetings. But apart from these spasmodic activities,
she exerted an insidious, incessant pressure upon the Emperor. There is no definite act, not even the declaration
of war in 1870, for which she can be made solely responsible. But her influence was great, and steadily on
the reactionary side. In the strictest sense of the term
she was not a *cléricale*, as were so many Spaniards and
Mexicans in her days: she did not follow blindly the
dictates of certain priests. But she was an ardent Catholic, and supported to the end the temporal power of the
Pope. The party she favored in Mexico was that of the
extreme conservatives, whose sole thought was to restore
the property, privileges, and absolute domination of the
Church. She resented as a personal affront the halting
evolution of the Empire toward liberalism. She did not
want the Émile Ollivier experiment to succeed: it seemed
to her that it would whittle down the prerogatives of her
son. She was among those who favored "a spirited attitude" in 1870: she trusted that a military victory would
enable the Empire to sweep away all liberal nonsense.
After the first defeats, she, against all competent authori-
ties, opposed the return of the Emperor to Paris: she
placed the prestige of the dynasty above the interests of
the nation.

Fifty years of dignified mourning blunted the resentment of the French: by treating her with deepening
respect, public opinion apologized indirectly to the whole
regime, so long unjustly damned without remission. But
she never understood the true nature of the Empire:

democratic Cæsarism. She did not realize that if Napoleon III used autocratic and repressive methods, it was
in the pursuit of a progressive policy.

Unfortunately, there was no one within the imperial
circle whose influence was capable of counterbalancing
that of Eugénie. I have already alluded to the oft-quoted
saying ascribed to Napoleon III, too neat to be authentic,
but strikingly accurate: "How can you expect the Empire to run straight? Eugénie is a Legitimist; Morny is
an Orléanist; my cousin Napoleon is a Republican; I
am a Socialist; there is but one Bonapartist in the lot,
Persigny; and *he* is mad." Morny, in so far as he was
anything, was an Orléanist: his ideal was a constitutional
monarchy run by the wealthy for the benefit of the
wealthy; the first and greatest commandment is: *"En-
richissez vous!"* And, in spite of his manifest gifts,
Prince Napoleon could not lead the left wing within the
imperial regime: his deplorable private life, his violent
temper, his irresponsibility, his rabid anticlericalism,
were insuperable disqualifications. Among the republicans, he never commanded confidence or respect. It is
highly to the credit of Napoleon III, enfeebled as he
was, that in the 1860's the Empire managed to steer its
appointed middle course without catastrophic reversals.
But for international problems, home difficulties might
have been surmounted: the Emperor won a great political victory as late as May 1870.

The first of these home difficulties came, not from
the radical opposition, but from those economic interests Napoleon III had served so well: the industrialists.
Ever since the days of Colbert, France had been fiercely
protectionist. The Emperor was inclined to free trade.
Not for doctrinaire reasons, but because he had seen

free trade in England increase the well-being of the
common man; because in his eyes free trade served the
cause of world peace; and because he wanted to
strengthen the ever precarious entente with England. A
Saint-Simonian whom he respected and liked, Michel
Chevalier, induced Richard Cobden to visit Paris. Secret negotiations were carried on at Saint-Cloud—an
economic Plombières. Then, early in 1860, a formal
treaty was signed, and in a very fine letter to Achille
Fould the Emperor expounded his liberal program. The
terms of the treaty were extremely moderate, but the opposition of the protectionists was bitter. Some industrial
establishments did suffer: England, with her wealth in
coal and her century-long experience in large-scale industry, had assets that France could hardly match. But
on the whole, and in spite of constant difficulties, French
industry went on expanding; and at the great Exposition
of 1867 it could show remarkable achievements. In this
case Napoleon III had proved that dream of the *Philosophes*: the Enlightened Despot.

Mere allusions must suffice for those distant activities
of the Empire which add little to our understanding of
the sovereign. France joined England in a punitive expedition against China. Punitive? But for the looting and
burning of the Summer Palace near Peking by the troops
of the civilizing powers there was no condign punish-
ment (1860). France alone, but as the mandatory of the
powers, conducted a brief police expedition in Syria,
where the Druses had massacred the Christian Maronites.
In both cases France acted as the protector of the
Church, the Temporal Sword in the service of Him who
had condemned the sword. Cochin China and Cam-
bodia became French possessions in 1862—the begin-

ning of that vast Indochinese Empire which the Fourth
Republic was to find it so difficult either to relinquish or
to defend. By methods of peaceful penetration, Faid-
herbe was turning a few trading posts in Senegal into the
nucleus of a vast West African dominion. About Algeria,
Napoleon III had saner views than many of his successors. He proclaimed himself "the Emperor of the Arabs
as well as of the French." He desired the peaceful co-
existence of the various elements, without subjection,
without forcible assimilation: in this he was the forerunner of Lyautey. He liberated Abd-el-Kader, the hero
of Algerian independence, and later made him Grand
Cross of the Legion of Honor. In an admirable portrait,
Hippolyte Flandrin painted Napoleon III peering into
the future: for the forward-looking, generosity is wisdom.

"Never has Liberty been able to build a lasting political structure; when time has consolidated the edifice,
Liberty crowns it." These words of Napoleon III, when
he opened the legislative session of 1853, were a blunt
assertion of authority; but they were also a promise.
When would the edifice be ready for its crown—in
years, decades, or centuries? Under the Third Republic,
the opportunist faith was summed up in two articles:
(1) "We must wait for the opportune moment." (2)
"The opportune moment may be tomorrow: it never is
today." Was the Bonapartist faith of the same slippery
kind?

In 1860 Napoleon III decided, not to establish a
liberal regime outright, but to start moving, by cautious
steps, in the direction of liberty. This evolution, during
the next ten years, was very real; but, like everything
else under that puzzling reign, it was ambiguous. It might

be considered as a sign of strength: the Empire was at
the height of its power; in the elections of 1857, only
five opponents had been returned. It could be considered
as an admission of bewilderment: the political problems
at home and abroad were getting beyond the grasp of
the ruler, and the misgivings of the people could no
longer be silenced. And both interpretations had their
measure of truth.

Second ambiguity: by liberalism, the bourgeoisie understood parliamentary rule, the free competition of parties, the omnipotence of an elected assembly. Even
today, rare are the minds free from such a confusion. To
Napoleon III, the rule of assemblies, as under Louis-
Philippe, was abomination: it meant the squabble of
factions, the chaos it was his mission to curb. Adolphe
Thiers thought that "liberty" meant the government of
Monsieur Thiers, under King or Emperor Log: Napoleon honestly believed that liberty meant liberation
from Monsieur Thiers and all the pettiness of which he
was such a perfect representative. Between the two conceptions there could be no sincere agreement. Even in
1870, when in weariness Napoleon III accepted a "constitutional"—that is, a parliamentary—regime, he reserved the principle of a direct appeal to the people,
the possibility of a legal *coup d'état* against the hucksters
and the prattlers. And the people responded as they had
in 1851. The ambiguity was never dispelled.

By the decree of November 24, 1860, the two
houses were allowed to discuss the terms of an address
in response to the speech from the throne. Thus, at the
opening of each session, there would be a survey of all
the problems that the country had to face. Proposed leg-
islation would be presented and defended before the legis-

lative body by "ministers without portfolios," as spokes-
men for the government; and the debates of the two
assemblies would henceforth be published in full. No
ministerial responsibility, the keystone of the parliamentary system: but there is none in America either. There
were at first three Ministers without Portfolios: Baroche,
Magne, Billault.

The elections of 1863 were hotly disputed. The government had a sweeping majority: six million against
two, very much the same figures as in the triumphal election of December 10, 1848. But Paris voted heavily
against the Empire, and Thiers, the arch-opponent of
the regime, was returned. Napoleon III was no
Charles X: he knew when to trim his sails. Persigny the
heavy-fisted was sacrificed, with a ducal coronet as a
parting gift. Duruy, a liberal historian, whom Napoleon
had found a congenial collaborator in his study of Cæsar,
became Minister of Public Education, almost a direct
challenge to the clerical party. Billault alone, as Minister
of State, remained the authorized mouthpiece of the Emperor.

The choice was excellent: Billault, a sincere supporter of the Empire, but no fanatic, had a cultured and
delicate mind, rich experience, and no lack of vigor. He
and Morny between them could give parliamentary debates at least a dignified semblance of activity without
endangering the principle of the regime: the Emperor
as full representative of the whole people. Unfortunately,
Billault died in October 1863, and Napoleon III pro-
moted his assistant Eugène Rouher to be his successor.

Eugène Rouher, a stocky, sturdy Auvergnat, had
done creditable work in high positions. No great orator,
he was a lucid, fluent, and at times all too forcible

speaker. His constant readiness and his indefatigable
vigor were, for the ailing and weary sovereign, a great
relief and a great temptation. Why not leave all the talk-
ing to Rouher? Napoleon III preserved the prerogative
of his imperial silence. So by degrees Rouher became,
not merely in the daily routine of affairs, but in matters
of high policy, the Vice-Emperor, and so he remained
for six fateful years. He was no fool, but his mind was
rough, and his temper bordered on vulgarity. The great
dreams, the far-sighted plans, the inveterate kindness of
the ruler were lost upon him. Because he had been given
quasi-supreme power, he believed in authority more than
the Emperor himself; in this he stood close to the Empress, who also enjoyed and defended jealously a position she had not created. Above all, Rouher had the
fundamental weakness of the lawyer and the politician:
he thought primarily of winning his case, from day to
day. A tactician, not a strategist. For all generous planning, he might have invented the term of contempt,
"starry-eyed."

Napoleon III at times chided him gently. When on
December 5, 1867 Rouher declared that *never* would
France allow Italy to enter Rome, the Emperor told
him: "In politics, Monsieur Rouher, one should never
say *never*." The master did as a rule preserve his fiery
agent from irreparable indiscretions, but the agent was
incapable of returning the same service. It was Rouher
who called the lamentable Mexican adventure "the
deepest thought of the reign."

Three problems, which overlapped and merged in-
extricably, beset the Empire in its second decade: the
Roman question from 1848 to 1870; the Mexican

embroilment from 1861 to 1867; the menace of Prussian hegemony in Germany and in Europe from 1864
to 1870. Each, complex in itself, was made worse confounded by the violent clashes of opinions at home.
Only totalitarian dictatorships can impose apparent unanimity; Napoleon's rule was dictatorial at times, it never
was totalitarian. Division is the badge, the glory, and the
peril of real freedom.

We have seen that in 1849 a French expedition destroyed Mazzini's Roman Republic and restored the
Pope. A determined show of force may veil hopeless
ambiguities. For the French republicans—and they still
controlled the National Assembly—the move was meant
to checkmate Austria, whose intervention would have
been the clear-cut triumph of reaction. According to the
Minister of Foreign Affairs, Drouyn de Lhuys, if the
Pope was to be restored, it was as a liberal ruler. And
the Prince-President upheld the same policy in a letter
to his friend Colonel Edgard Ney. But the murder of
his minister Rossi and the insurrection against his own
paternal rule had made "liberalism" in any form abhor-
rent to Pius IX. Henceforth he was to be the standard-
bearer of Christian society against the Red menace to
God, Legitimacy, and Property. The French conservatives, who had helped elect the President, and who came
to full power on May 28, 1849, were in complete accord with the Pope. They considered the Roman expedition their triumph. The temporal power of the Papacy
became the symbol of conservatism throughout Europe.
What France needed was "a Roman expedition at
home."

For ten years the situation remained at the same time
tense and dormant. Then came the Italian campaign.

Napoleon III, a genuine Italian patriot, hoped for the liberation and unification of the whole peninsula, but in the form of a federation, with the Pope, retaining his own territories, as its president. Between modern and liberal Piedmont on the one hand, the Two Sicilies and the Papal States on the other, no close association was possible: they belonged to different centuries. Napoleon's far-sighted and peaceful plan was rejected by unanimous tacit consent. So the minor principalities freely united with Piedmont, the northeastern provinces of the Papal States seceded, Garibaldi conquered Sicily and Naples. The Pope was now besieged in his woefully reduced domain, under the protection of French arms.

This was a great victory for the liberals, the Reds, the enemies of God and of society—the terms were then interchangeable. And the Emperor had done nothing to stop this sacrilegious spoliation; he may even have nodded approval. The French conservatives, for many years the faithful supporters of the Empire, were infuriated. The bishops uttered, or rather fulminated, their most solemn warnings. If the Empire was not to forfeit their loyalty, the French army must remain in Rome.

On September 15, 1864 Napoleon III came to a reasonable compromise with the new Kingdom of Italy. Rome would be respected. Florence was to be the capital. The French army would be withdrawn within two years. The Pope considered this agreement as a betrayal of his sacred rights, as a victory for the revolutionary spirit. On December 8 he replied with a virulent denunciation of all liberal tendencies, in two great documents, the encyclical *Quanta Cura*, and the *Syllabus of the Errors of Our Age*. The eightieth and last proposition of the *Syllabus* is a memorable challenge: "Anathema on him who should ever maintain: that the Pontiff can and must be reconciled and compromise with progress, liberalism, and modern civilization."

We must constantly repeat that for Napoleon III, order was not an ideal *per se,* and was not identical with conservatism: it was a condition of progress. Thus the *Syllabus* was condemning the policy of the Emperor root and branch. He met the attack with the same vigorous methods he had used against his opponents of the Left: the publication of the *Syllabus* in France was forbidden, and Catholic newspapers felt in their turn the weight of censorship. The battle was engaged on every plane: in the realm of ideas, in diplomacy, in home politics. But the three-cornered fight was extraordinarily confused. Napoleon III still considered himself a good Catholic and the protector of the Church; so he was considered by many believers; and he was denounced for this very reason by the anticlericals, his cousin Napoleon in the lead.

In December 1866, in accordance with the agreement, the last French troops were withdrawn from Rome. The Pope did not rely for his security entirely on the good faith of the Italian King. During the two years' respite, the Papal army had been reorganized. It drew volunteers from the whole Catholic world, and was placed under the command of a French general— a bitter opponent of the Empire—Lamoricière. But on October 27, 1867 the irrepressible Garibaldi attacked what remained of the Papal States. The French had prepared for such a contingency: immediately they landed again at Civita Vecchia. On November 3 they defeated Garibaldi at Mentana. This victory was a day of

shame and mourning for the French liberals. They were
not comforted by the report that "the new Chassepot
rifles had done wonders." As the Kingdom of Italy had
been unable to restrain the great condottiere, the French
stayed in Rome. They were still there when the Franco-
Prussian War broke out.

Napoleon III then dispatched his cousin Prince Napoleon on a mission to his father-in-law, Victor Emmanuel II. The Italian King did not refuse to honor the
terms of the alliance, but he named his price: Rome.
The Empress haughtily rejected the proposal. She was
a conservative and could not abandon a key position.
She was a Catholic, and the Pope was her son's god-
father. When his offer was rejected, Victor Emmanuel
felt greatly relieved: Prussia too had been his ally, and
more recently than France. On August 19 the French
left Rome at last. On September 4 the Empire fell. On
September 20 the Italian troops entered Rome, meeting only with a token resistance. On October 20 the
Vatican Council closed after having proclaimed the
dogma of Papal infallibility.

The Mexican adventure has been described as a grab
that failed. While the police were fighting among themselves, the imperial burglar attempted to loot a helpless
country. When the police returned to duty, he dropped
the swag and slunk away.

This picture is another caricature; like all caricatures,
it has a painful element of truth. Again, reality offers an
infinitely complex blend: greed and noble dreams, far-
sighted plans and sheer gambles, the whole smothered in
blundering. The affair began in a commonplace way.

In 1861 the Mexican government had to suspend payment on its foreign obligations. By the Treaty of London, on October 31, France, Great Britain, and Spain decided to act jointly for the protection of their interests; on December 17 they occupied Vera Cruz.

Napoleon III would not have moved single-handed. But the entente among the three powers did not last long. Some of the French claims (the Jecker Bonds, with the backing of Morny) were outrageous. England was averse to any intervention of a political character. The Spanish representative, General Prim, a soldier with illimitable ambitions, expected to have command of the allied forces; when this was denied him, he withdrew. France was left alone.

Her aims were ill-defined. Officially, she was still pursuing (*manu militari*) a purely financial understanding with President Juárez. By agreement, the occupation troops had been allowed, while discussions were proceeding, to camp inland, away from the fever-ridden marshes of the coast. A ticklish situation: minor conflicts were hard to avoid. The French general, Lorencez, ill advised by Mexican conservatives and by a war-minded diplomat, Dubois de Saligny, advanced to the gates of Puebla. On May 5, 1862 he was checked by the *juaristas* and compelled to fall back upon Orizaba.

France so far had not been aware that she was engaged in a serious contest in Mexico. The opposition, ably led by Jules Favre, warned the government of the dangers. But, according to the deplorable tradition of military prestige, it was impossible to withdraw after a defeat: the humiliation of Puebla must first be avenged. Credits were voted, and a veritable army was shipped to

Vera Cruz under General Forey. Billault, the Minister
of State, spoke only of the honor of the flag: no mention was made of a proposed Mexican Empire.

But the thought had already entered the minds both
of the Emperor and of the Empress. Only it was two
different empires they had in view. The only point the
two had in common was that neither had a basis in actual facts.

Eugénie had been won over by the Mexican exiles,
Gutierrez de Estrada, Hidalgo, Almonte, Monsignor
Labastida. They were radically opposed to the whole
reforma movement, and particularly to the measures that
had curbed the power and cut down the possessions of
the clergy. They claimed that in Mexico, an ardently
Catholic country, the agitators who had disturbed the
social edifice were but a handful. The merest show of
force would rally the oppressed or deluded masses to
the righteous cause.

Napoleon III caressed the idea of an empire in the
image of his own: a regime that would restore order so
as to foster progress. He was a democrat in his own
fashion: he was not a republican. Republics had failed
in France, as they were failing everywhere in Latin
America. Even in the United States the Civil War was
making it plain that republican institutions were not a
panacea. The only American country that was develop-
ing in peace was Brazil, under an enlightened Emperor.
Napoleon III considered himself as the appointed leader
of the "Latin" world. He wanted to strengthen that vast
area against the "colossus of the North," which, fourteen years earlier, had wrested from Mexico half of its
territory. The North American reader may be pardoned
for viewing events in a different perspective. But Na-

poleon III's conception had no lack of consistency. In our own days the Mexican José Vasconcelos, a brilliant mind, recognized its merits.

Empress and Emperor agreed upon a candidate: Archduke Maximilian, brother of Francis Joseph. Both wanted to compensate the Habsburgs for their loss of prestige in Italy, Napoleon moved by his inveterate desire for the healing of wounds, Eugénie, because she had a predilection for Austria as the ideal Catholic and legitimist state. Maximilian was young, handsome, not inexperienced: he had done well as Viceroy in Milan, and he was eager to prove his mettle. His wife, Charlotte, daughter of Leopold, King of the Belgians, was even more dazzled by the prospect of an imperial crown in a land of exotic romance. Maximilian, however, set conditions that were extremely sound: that he be called by the manifest desire of the Mexican people; and that he be assured of the support, not of France merely, but of England and Spain as well.

Meanwhile Forey, after staying in winter quarters at Orizaba, had marched upon Puebla in March 1863. The siege was protracted and costly; when the French fought their way into the battered city, they found the "liberated" population unresponsive and even sullen. A different reception, however, awaited them in Mexico City, from which Juárez had fled. On June 10 they entered the capital "on a carpet of flowers" amid the joyous ringing of the bells and the acclaim of the populace. Deluded by this brave show, Forey hastened to turn over the government to a junta of conservatives. They in their turn picked out an Assembly of Notables, all of the same persuasion. It was this highly misrepresentative body that offered the crown to Maximilian.

The archduke and the French Emperor must have known that this was no honest plebiscite. At one time Napoleon hesitated on the brink; at another, Maximilian. But each held the other to his promise, and both accepted the calculated risk: if this was *not yet* the spontaneous wish of the Mexican people, the presence of an Emperor might be a decisive element. It almost came to pass: when Maximilian reached Mexico City on June 10, 1864, a year after the French troops had entered it, he and his consort were wildly acclaimed.

Forey returned to France with a marshal's baton; Bazaine succeeded him. With far fewer soldiers than Lyautey, half a century later, had in Morocco, he "pacified" the vast country in little over one year. Juárez was driven to El Paso; only guerrillas kept up the resistance. Maximilian felt justified in considering them as bandits: if caught in arms, they were to be summarily shot.

The political situation, however, was hopeless. Wherever they went, the imperial pair was cheered, and Maximilian may have had vaguely liberal ideas, although he was far more interested in court etiquette. But he found himself the prisoner of the ultra-reactionaries, who had not called him from Miramar Castle to be a crowned Juárez. The intelligent middle class—a very scant element in the Mexico of the last century—when not outright pro-Juárez, was discouraged by the clerical tinge of the governing circles. Harassed and bankrupt, Mexico had no funds to spare for a vast program of public works.

The decisive blows, however, were not struck in Mexico itself. As soon as the Civil War was over, the United States insisted on the withdrawal of the French troops: intervention may wear different colors, and 1865 was not 1778. Napoleon, harried by fierce opposition at home, had to face menacing European problems. He understood. On January 15, 1866 he notified Maximilian that he would recall his army. There was ample time for the Mexican Emperor to retire: a mistaken sense of honor and duty, the dread of creeping back defeated to an ironical Europe, bade him remain. He and Charlotte even thought that they would at last find their way to their people's hearts, now that the overbearing and ruthless Bazaine was leaving. They soon realized their pathetic impotence. Charlotte rushed to Paris, pleaded in vain, scolded, raged, and finally took refuge in madness, not to be released until death, sixty years later. On March 12, 1867 Bazaine left Vera Cruz. On June 19 Maximilian was shot at Querétaro.

Napoleon III was "a man of '48," much closer to Mazzini than he was to Bismarck. He had hoped for a Europe in which problems could be settled by international congresses in the light of far-sighted and generous principles. That hope was waning. Nationalism, at first a gospel of fraternity, was turning into a tribal spirit, fierce and exclusive. Science, far from bringing "sweetness and light," was spreading materialistic darkness. Darwinism was interpreted as "struggle for life." This was called "realism" in philosophy, art, and politics, and Bismarck, the master of *Realpolitik*, was soon to proclaim that international problems were to be settled through blood and iron.

In the case of Poland, Napoleon III was sadly impressed with the impotence of his ideal. Like most Frenchmen, he felt that as long as the martyrdom of Poland endured, Europe was in a state of mortal sin.

When an insurrection broke out in 1863, all hearts were
with the Polish patriots: for once, Napoleon and the
Empress were on the same side. The Emperor was
urged to intervene. But what could he do? England refused to support even his most cautious diplomatic
moves. Mere diplomacy would have been futile; a war
of the liberal West against Poland's three jailers would
have caused more sufferings than it could have relieved.
The sole results of Napoleon III's velleities were a
sense of frustration and the cooling of Franco-Russian
relations.

In 1864 the problem of the duchies broke out again.
Schleswig and Holstein were in an ambiguous position.
They were under the Danish crown, but they were also
part of the vague Germanic confederacy. A large pro-
portion of the population spoke German. Austria and
Prussia waged war on hapless Denmark. This time England wanted some action: her sympathies were with the
royal Danish house. Moated by the sea, she was in-
vulnerable: all the perils of a conflict with the Central
Powers would have fallen upon France. Napoleon III
sadly shook his head. He could only get into the peace
treaty a stipulation for a plebiscite, his favorite device.
This promise was not redeemed until 1920, when North
Schleswig was returned to Denmark.

Austria was the traditional head of the Germanic
Confederacy, tenuous shadow of the shadowy Holy Roman Empire. Her supremacy had been rudely challenged by Frederick the Great in the eighteenth century.
After the War of Liberation (1813-5), Prussia,
stretching from Memel to Malmédy, could no longer
be held in subordination. Austria was a multi-national
empire; she was Catholic rather than German; and her

rule, especially under the interminable Metternich regime, had been frankly antagonistic to progress. Even
the Frankfurt Parliament had found it hard to define the
place of Austria in the Germanic body.

The struggle for supremacy came to a head in 1866.
It was startlingly brief: after seven weeks Austria was
decisively defeated at Königgrätz (Sadowa). Napoleon III had expected a protracted struggle. In case of a
stalemate, his mediation would have been welcome:
once more he would have been the arbiter of Europe.
The swift and absolute triumph of Prussia destroyed
that flattering possibility.

When the news of Sadowa reached Paris, the first
reaction was favorable. Austrians were well liked in
France, but Austria was an inveterate enemy. France
still wanted to follow Richelieu's injunction: "Humili-
ate the House of Austria." The liberals far preferred
modern, efficient, scientific Prussia. Bismarck, huge,
handsome, bluff, and witty, a thorough diplomat under
his artful bluntness, had been very popular at the Tuileries. It must be noted that Napoleon had encouraged
Victor Emmanuel to ally himself with Prussia: he
wanted, in fulfillment of his pledge in 1859, Italy to
have Venice. So a number of people in Paris, spon-
taneously, lighted Chinese lanterns as a time-honored
sign of rejoicing.

Their reaction was not unsound: had France fully
accepted the situation, the unity of Germany under Prussian leadership would have offered no threat to her
essential interests. Although some Germans had been
clamoring for Alsace since 1813, Bismarck was not committed to that policy. Then the mood changed from
cheerful equanimity to sullenness, as though a word had

been passed: Sadowa appeared as an intolerable humiliation for France. The opposition, of course, played that
card. Sadowa undeniably involved a loss of prestige:
the Prussians, those upstarts, had dared to conquer without consulting France. And their victory shattered the
hope of settling once for all, in a manner acceptable to
French pride, the eternal problem of the Rhine frontier.
In 843, by the Treaty of Verdun, Charlemagne's empire had been partitioned among his three grandsons.
And for one thousand years France and Germany, as
they slowly grew into national consciousness, had been
wrestling for the amorphous zone between them, the
share of Lothair: Lotharingia. Had Austria been victorious, a buffer state, thoroughly German but friendly
to France, might have been created in the Rhineland.

Napoleon III had no cause and no desire to fight the
victor—who had just demonstrated his marvelous efficiency. But the ultra-Bonapartists and the opposition
harped so much on France's loss of prestige that the Emperor felt compelled to seek some compensation. His
mediation was accepted, but only after the terms of
peace had been incorporated in the armistice. Venice
was yielded to him, and he generously turned it over
to Italy. But Europe smiled incredulously, and Italy,
smarting under her defeats at Custozza and Lissa, resented the slur that this indirect cession implied. In October 1865 Napoleon had conducted secret negotiations
with Bismarck at Biarritz; it was expected that some
agreement had resulted from this other Plombières. But
the discussions had proved abortive. Napoleon III had
reached the point of mental fatigue when he could not
think clearly of bridges ahead, and when he came to the
river of decision, there was no bridge at all.

After Sadowa, he hinted at modest compensations: Mayence? The Palatinate? The Sarre? At least those few cities in the Sarre that had remained French until 1814, and had not been wrenched from her until after Waterloo? Bismarck scornfully called these hesitant overtures "begging for a tip." The victor saw no reason to yield an inch of German soil for services not rendered. These minor rebuffs rankled. France was confirmed in the belief that Sadowa had been a great national disaster.

A last chance came. The King of the Netherlands was willing to sell to France the Grand Duchy of Luxemburg, which was his personal possession. A plebiscite would probably have ratified the transaction: the upper classes were to a large extent Frenchified; the common people, speaking a local dialect, had no national German feeling; and the France of 1867, in spite of recent rebuffs, still enjoyed incomparable glamour. Unfortunately, the city of Luxemburg happened to be a federal German fortress. Its transfer to France would have been a humiliation for a nation "in process of becoming," and bursting with pride and hope. It was impossible for Bismarck not to interpose his veto. For a while the situation was threatening. Ultimately a compromise was reached. The duchy was made independent and neutral; it would join the North German *Zollverein*, or customs union; the fortress was to be dismantled. A wan and weary peace might still be nursed back to health.

CHAPTER EIGHT

IN DUBIOUS BATTLE
1867–1870

"We shall give the Emperor a happy old age."

—ÉMILE OLLIVIER

OUR last chapter must have left with the reader an impression of unmitigated gloom. This could hardly be avoided: in such a brief sketch as this, it is difficult to render all the dissolving lights and shades. In 1867, many observers saw no reason to believe that the Empire was doomed. Its prestige had suffered, but prestige is an elusive thing. It may vanish with dramatic suddenness and never return; it may survive many checks and rebuffs; it may even revive after an eclipse. The moral leadership of America went through feverish rises and falls during the decade that followed the end of the Second World War. The prestige of Byzantium, that of the Holy Roman Empire, that of Spain, had an interminable twilight. In the nineteenth century, Austria suffered repeated humiliations; yet it remained, not only a going concern, but an impressive great power. As late as 1914, it still had a chance of creating and leading a Danubian Federation.

On more practical ground than prestige, France in 1867 had enjoyed fifteen years of order and prosperity. Not without shadows and misgivings, to be sure. But the wealth of the country was no dream, and no permanent loss of momentum was perceptible. The economy of France was still dynamic.

Finally, although the Emperor had lost his aura of miraculous luck, although the deterioration of his health and will power was known to a few and surmised by many, it was felt that the regime, just because it was a hybrid, was capable of renovation. With dimmer sight and enfeebled hand, the Emperor was still attempting to discern the state of public opinion and to shape his course according to its trend. There had been recessions on several fronts, but no irretrievable loss.

In the year 1867 splendor and anguish offered a tragic and baroque contrast. The reconstruction of Paris, the most sensational achievement of the Empire, was in its main lines completed. The great Exposition, admirably planned by the Catholic sociologist Le Play, was immensely larger and more brilliant than that of 1855. It revealed the industrial development of the age; and in quality if not in bulk, France could hold her own against England or Germany. Princes, kings, emperors, entertained three and five at a time, seemed to pay court to their overlord. Napoleon's ingrained desire for reconciliation was satisfied: the King of Prussia came and was well received. Never had the glamour of Parisian life enjoyed such a universal appeal. Aristocrats, wits, and *philosophes* flocked to the eighteenth-century *salons* in their hundreds; but now farmers and merchants, athirst for a more brilliant and freer life, came in their myriads from the ends of the world.

No doubt there was a meretricious aspect to this pleasure rush. The Brazilians and Moldo-Wallachians who booked theater seats months in advance did not wish to see *Polyeucte* or *Athalie,* but *La Vie Parisienne,* and Hortense Schneider in *La Grande-Duchesse de Gerolstein.* It was Theresa the irreverent gamine whom they

wanted to hear, not Renan or Claude Bernard. Luxury
and power were evident everywhere, with a glow of
intelligence and a gloss of taste that saved them from
utter vulgarity. But there were hints of decay, as in a
golden autumnal landscape. The new Paris was impressive, but its energetic creator, Haussmann, was under
bitter attack. If the Exposition was a breath-taking epit-
ome of man's efforts, it offered a fringe of pleasure re-
sorts which made material progress seem vain and even
perilous. If the playboys—*lions* and *cocodès*—had their
fling, the temper of many old families, the mainstay of
France, was critical and even sullen. Everywhere, by
the side of vigor and confidence, there could be felt a
sense of uneasy satiety, of restless torpor, of undefinable
dread. Ernest Hello, the Catholic mystic, wondered
prophetically why the Tuileries were not yet ablaze and
why the Barbarians should so long delay their coming.
In my own youth the splendors of 1867 were still un-
forgotten; to many thoughtful contemporaries they
seemed entrancing and oppressive, like some gorgeous
and feverish dream.

These contrasts may be summed up in one scene. On
June 30 the imperial family was to preside over the dis-
tribution of prizes at the Exposition. Two historical
stagecoaches, all crystal and gold, straight from the land
of Cinderella and the Trianon Museum, with eight
horses apiece, carried the Emperor, the Empress, the
Prince Imperial, and the guest of honor, the Sultan.
Among those present was the Prince of Wales. The
Prince Imperial, eleven years old, gave out the prizes
as nominal President of the Exposition and mascot of the
regime. His playing the star role gave a touch of sentiment to a very humdrum and fatiguing occasion: the

vast audience was sweltering in that magnified hothouse, the Palace of Industry. Hardly had the twelve-hundred-piece orchestra struck up an anthem by Rossini when an aide handed the Emperor a telegram. The sovereign remained impassive, went on with the show, gave a speech on peace, progress, good will. But the Austrian Ambassador and his staff quietly withdrew. The message confirmed the news of Maximilian's death.

Napoleon III was not blind to the Prussian menace. More than prestige was at stake. The advent of Bismarck was a portent: resurgent barbarism ("blood and iron") with all the resources of modern technique. It was no longer a question of conquering the left bank of the Rhine, but of preserving the integrity and dignity of France.

To meet that threat, two means were necessary: a network of alliances, and a larger, more efficient army. The Emperor addressed himself to both tasks; in both he came tantalizingly near success.

He had always sought the friendship and co-operation of England—at times against the grumblings of his followers. By 1867 he had long been aware that he could never count on full-hearted British support. Queen Victoria had been won by the strange personality of Napoleon III, and especially by his unexpected gentleness, but politically she never was a friend. Her origins were German; her beloved Albert had been the quintessence of Germanism; her daughter was Crown Princess of Prussia. Protestant England disliked Napoleon as the protector of the Pope, and felt in sympathy with Lutheran North Germany. Pro-Germanism assumed a virulent form in Carlyle, who was considered by many as a genius and a major prophet. The best that could be expected of Russia was frigid neutrality: the Polish problem created a gulf between Russia and France, a bond of complicity between Russia and Prussia. Austria and Italy alone offered serious chances of support.

Napoleon III did his best to win their friendship. No easy task. Austria, herself in the throes of reorganization, could hardly be brought into the same camp as Italy, with whom she had fought twice in seven years. And between Italy and France the Roman question was a constant source of distrust and enmity. Above all, both Austria and Italy had been impressed by the scientific efficiency of the Prussian army. Nations are shy of linking their fate with a power doomed to defeat: like Mussolini in 1940, they prefer rushing to the assistance of the victor. So Austria and Italy would consider an alliance with France only if two conditions were fulfilled: that the regime should offer guarantees of stability, and that its military establishment be greatly improved.

The key even to the diplomatic situation therefore was army reform. In September 1866 France had under arms 288,000 men: a third of them stationed in Rome, Algeria, Mexico. No organized reserves. The Germanic Confederation could bring into line 1,100,000 trained soldiers. The French army was theoretically based on universal military duty, but not on universal military service. The contingent, determined every year, was far less than the number of young men coming of age. Lots were drawn; those who had an unlucky number had to serve seven years; the rest were completely released from further obligations. And—this was the crux of the whole problem—if a young bourgeois was drafted, he could purchase a substitute. The rich therefore were never found in the ranks. They could choose a military career as officers; or they could keep out of the army altogether. This privilege they were determined to defend with heroic obstinacy.

In October and November 1866 Napoleon III convened a special commission composed of the marshals, a few high-ranking generals, his right-hand man Rouher, and some cabinet ministers. He proposed effective universal service for a limited term. Prince Napoleon alone supported him. The generals were not enthusiastic. Trained reserves—disguised civilians—did not appeal to them. If you want a larger army, said the Minister of War, Randon, why not raise the term of service from seven to nine years? All, especially Marshal Vaillant, a political-minded soldier, warned the Emperor that his scheme would encounter implacable hostility in the Chamber. Napoleon knew that even a referendum on the subject would turn against him. Discouraged, he accepted the compromise plan of Marshal Niel, whom he then made his Minister of War: all Frenchmen to serve for six years, with the colors or in the reserve; as a goal, 1,200,000 trained or in training; 400,000 on active service, 400,000 in the reserve, 400,000 in the territorial guard.

Marshal Niel, long Napoleon's confidential adviser, was an excellent choice. Not a *beau sabreur*, but a serious student of military problems, he was intelligent, firm and not intransigent. But public opinion was almost unanimous against his plan. The prefects reported widespread discontent; by-elections showed sudden gains in opposition votes. Even loyal Bonapartists vowed that if they had to vote for the law in deference to the Emperor's wishes, they would see to it that it was sabotaged.

Everyone hated the thought of a sharp increase in the military burden. The bourgeois would not give up their cherished prerogative not to serve. The republicans were only too glad to oppose the government on any issue. Besides, they were pursuing most sincerely a lofty ideal of peace and disarmament, of which Victor Hugo was the pontiff. What if France herself were invaded? Then they would call *la levée en masse,* all Frenchmen rising invincibly to the defense of the sacred soil, as in 1793.

To accept Niel's plan had been a first capitulation. Now Niel had to capitulate in his turn before the fierce opposition of Chamber and country. The worst elements of the old system were retained: the contingent to be fixed every year, men for active service to be chosen by lot, the rich still able to buy themselves off. The territorial guard (*Garde Mobile*) remained merely a name. The sole important change was that the term of service was reduced from seven years to five. Instead of being enlarged and revitalized, the French army actually lost some of its striking power.

This might have been wisdom, if public opinion had pursued a determined policy of peace. But all parties had united in upbraiding the Empire for loss of prestige and lack of spirit. Throughout the reign the republicans, apostles of peace, had clamored for democratic crusades, for tearing up the *Diktat* of Vienna, for reconquering the "natural and historical frontiers." As for the middle class, I must quote again Doudan's pungent remark: "The French bourgeois wants to 'bestrew with his corpse' all the battlefields of Europe, while toasting his toes by his cozy fireside." In a more modern phrase, he wanted butter first of all, but also the prestige and power that demand the backing of big guns.

Napoleon III drew the lesson: if the French had no desire to rearm, then they should be resolved not to fight. He adopted a passive line of conduct, well in accord with his own fatigue. "What does it matter?" he answered in 1870, when they proposed Gramont as Foreign Secretary; "he or some other, since we have decided to do nothing?" He, the Man on Horseback, the heir of the Napoleonic Legend, was thus forced into the attitude of Louis-Philippe: make as good a show as you can, but pursue a policy of peace-at-any-price. If two had played at that game, it would have been safe enough. But Bismarck had his own aims and his own methods.

1867 had been a year of violent contrasts: the Franco-Prussian conflict tense to the breaking-point, peace preserved without dishonor, the splendors, both glitter and gold, of the Exposition; the humiliation and the remorse of Maximilian's death. 1868 was a year of dull, unrelieved, mounting irritation. The Exposition had left a hangover: it had raised the cost of living, it had not created permanent sources of prosperity. Now the crops were poor and business was stagnant. The government attempted to assuage this discontent by accelerating the liberal reforms. The press laws were to be greatly relaxed; public meetings, even of a purely political nature, were to be made much easier. The Bonapartists of the Old Guard grumbled; Persigny, now in ducal retirement, foresaw the inevitable end: what is Bonapartism if not a government with a grip? The Empress was dismayed by this yielding to the forces of subversion. Anticlericalism in particular was rife, as the occupation of Rome was the weakest point in the Emperor's policy; and Eugénie associated in her mind God, the Pope, and the Empire. Even the Vice-Emperor Rouher disapproved of the trend. He offered to retire; Napoleon III, dreading too radical a change, induced him to remain. Rouher, a retained advocate, did defend before the Chamber the proposed measures, and on one occasion, at least, he defended them well. But his heart was on the other side.

These concessions were wise; indeed, they were long overdue. But they could not retrieve the popularity and increase the strength of the regime. What the people really wanted was not so much the right to voice their discontent as positive remedies for their uneasiness. A show of dynamism on the part of the government would have helped far more than any "liberal" law. But the men in power had nothing to offer in that line: no foreign adventure, no Mexico with illimitable prospects; even public works, railroad-building, city improvements, had leveled off and were beginning to offer diminishing returns. The Suez Canal was nearing completion, but it provided employment only for a handful of French engineers. The opposition, either clerical, or bourgeois Orléanist, or republican, had no constructive program to offer either. So the new liberties could be used for destructive purposes only, to criticize more bitterly the existing regime.

The immediate result was a great increase in virulence; that is to say, in vulgarity. The imperial censorship had at least imposed a degree of decency in tone. Even the Five, the able and courageous republican minority in the lower house since 1857, had spoken with studied moderation. Now the flood gates of scurrility were open. Hundreds imitated Victor Hugo's apocalyptic vehemence, without the least shadow of his all-absolving genius. Modern readers may well be astounded at the tremendous success of Rochefort's weekly pamphlet, *La Lanterne* (from May 30, 1868). An impoverished aristocrat, the Marquis Henri de Rochefort-Luçay, had written chatty columns, at the same time bright and vapid, for the more frivolous smart-set papers. He saw his chance, and turned his methods—personal insults spiced with wisecracks—to the destruction of the regime. The response was prodigious.

In July 1868 Eugène Ténot published his *Paris en Décembre 1851*. It exposed the acts of brutality which had marked and marred the *Coup d'Etat;* its success was another blow to the Empire. In its pages, the republicans rediscovered a forgotten hero, Dr. Baudin. Delescluze opened a subscription for a monument to the man whom the Parisian workers had refused to follow. The subscription was going none too well, when the government committed the blunder of prosecuting Delescluze. He was defended by Léon Gambetta. The trial gave the bohemian young lawyer a splendid opportunity to display his impassioned southern eloquence. Jules Favre was aging, Ollivier ready to turn his coat; Gambetta, ardent, untrammeled, untried, appealed to the new generation. Overnight, the hero of Left Bank cafés found himself a national leader; and, miraculously, there was a statesman's mind back of the turgid words. Napoleon III himself remarked: "This Gambetta is a man of great talent," just as Leo X had said of Luther: "Brother Martin has genius."

The general elections of May 23–4, 1869, the fourth since Napoleon had assumed full power, were held after a campaign of unlimited freedom and incredible violence. The first returns were appalling: at the

Tuileries, Emperor and Empress were struck with consternation. All the great cities, Paris in the lead, had declared themselves against the Empire. The final results,
when the solid rural masses had been counted, mitigated
the gloom: 4,438,000 had voted for the government,
3,355,000 against. Under a parliamentary regime such
a majority would have been counted a substantial victory. The aim of the Empire, however, had been to
unite all Frenchmen on essential issues: a divided vote
meant a return to the party system, in abeyance for eighteen years.

Cæsarism had lost its magic. Yet it was impossible for
the Emperor to quit. Technically, he had scored a victory. He could not turn the government over to an opposition that was not even a loose coalition. Legitimists,
Orléanists, moderate Republicans, Radicals, Socialists,
had nothing in common but their distrust of the imperial
regime. Once more Napoleon had to seek the component of these many divergent forces. A delicate task, for
the Bonapartists were hardly less divided than their opponents. Rouher and the Empress still advocated strong-
arm methods. Persigny, the earliest and most active of
Napoleon's lieutenants, had finally learned his lesson,
and publicly gave excellent advice: "Let the Emperor
persevere in the ways of liberalism. But let him seek
support among the new generations. The men of December 2nd, like myself, are through."

There came vaguely into existence a "third party,"
professing loyalty to the regime, but definitely parliamentary in spirit. Napoleon was reluctant to give up
Rouher, who, for all his shortcomings, was vigorous and
devoted. Still the lesson of May 24 was unequivocal,
and Rouher was not the man for the new policy. So the

Vice-Emperor himself read to the Chamber the list of reforms that the sovereign was planning; then he sent in his resignation. With the proper sense of humor, Napoleon III did *not* make him a duke (July 13).

A colorless transitional cabinet was formed, headed by Forcade la Roquette. The obvious candidate for the premiership was Adolphe Thiers. France evidently desired to try the parliamentary method again, and Thiers was the Grand Old Man of that system. Although an Orléanist, he had closely collaborated with the Republicans in 1863 and 1869. And as early as 1864 he had manifested his willingness to work with the Empire, if only "the five indispensable liberties" were secured. But we should never forget that Thiers stood for everything that Napoleon had sought to curb or destroy: the party spirit, the sanctity of private greed, the unquestioned rule of the propertied middle class. Napoleon believed in social democratic Cæsarism, Thiers was a hater of "the vile multitude." To accept him would have been for Napoleon III not merely capitulation, but treason.

Besides, Thiers was seventy-two; he had been in active politics since 1830; and Napoleon heeded Persigny's advice: govern with the new generation. The coming man was Émile Ollivier, forty-four years of age, in the fullness of his powers. He was untried, but not inexperienced: thanks to his father, Démosthène Ollivier, he had held public office as early as 1848. An ardent Republican, he had become one of the famous Five (Favre, Ollivier, Hénon, Darimon, Picard) who had courageously represented the opposition in the Chamber. But as early as 1860 Morny had discerned in him an opportunist or pragmatist democrat who, without sacrificing his convictions, could be brought to co-operate

with the Empire. After the "liberal" decrees of 1860,
Morny asked him: "Are you satisfied?" and Ollivier
answered: "If you mean to go no farther, you are lost;
if this is just a beginning, you are saved." The death of
Morny, the ascendancy of Rouher, retarded Ollivier's
hour. At the end of 1866 Walewski unofficially offered him a ministerial post, which he declined. By
1869, the old Republicans, like Carnot, Favre, Raspail,
and the new radical generation, like Gambetta, were
aware that, without any formal break, he was no longer
one of them.

Ollivier was eloquent, but no windbag: he was capable of serious study and steadfast work. He was a
man of culture, at home in literary and artistic circles:
his first wife was the daughter of Liszt and the Countess
d'Agoult. Of a kindly and cheerful disposition, he could
not, like Hugo, be one of God's angry men. He had
never hated Napoleon III; when he came to work with
him, bonds of genuine affection were created between
the two men. Ollivier was known to address his sovereign, against all etiquette, as "My dear Sire." Morny,
with better rights, had called him "My dear Emperor."
Thiers, in the eyes of Napoleon III, would have meant
a relapse; Ollivier was something of an adventure. And,
racked with disease or numb with opiates, the inveterate
imperial gambler was glad to play a new card.

While negotiations were afoot in Paris for the forma-
tion of the new ministry, the Empire was enjoying, two
thousand miles away, its most brilliant and best-deserved
hour of triumph. On November 16–19 the Suez Canal
was inaugurated. It had been almost wholly a French
enterprise, carried out against the indifference and even
the hostility of England. The Emperor could not be

spared from his political duties; so it was the Empress who represented the country. This was particularly appropriate, as Ferdinand de Lesseps was a cousin of hers, and she had supported him in moments of desperate difficulties. As at the Congress of Paris in 1856, as during a golden week in 1867, the Empire appeared in a position of friendly and courteous pre-eminence. The Khedive of Egypt—a lavish host—the Emperor of Austria, the Prince Royal of Prussia, the Prince and Princess of the Netherlands, the Emir Abd-el-Kader, a dazzling array of ministers and diplomats, an élite of writers, artists, scientists, journalists, seemed to form the retinue of the French sovereign, who, still strikingly beautiful in her full maturity, was radiant with pride and happiness. The imperial yacht *L'Aigle* led the long procession from Port Said to Suez. The canal had been one of the dreams of those very practical utopians, the disciples of Saint-Simon; and Napoleon III, "Saint-Simon on horseback," had willed and helped its realization.

The new constitution created by the reforms of 1869—for although it still preserved the 1852 façade, it was new in its spirit—came very close to the English ideal of parliamentary government. There were traces of personal rule: officially there was no prime minister, and the cabinet members were responsible to the Emperor alone. The old Cæsarian leopard was proud of his spots, and extremely reluctant to change them. The Senate, long a luxurious Home for the Loyal and Illustrious Aged, became an upper house, with the same rights as the Chamber. At last the stopgap administration of Forcade la Roquette was swept aside. On December 27, 1869 Napoleon formally asked Ollivier to form a cabinet "faithfully representing the majority." On the 2nd of January 1870 that cabinet officially came into being. Ollivier was Minister of Justice (Keeper of the Seals). Daru was entrusted with Foreign Affairs, Buffet with Finances: two very sound, respected men. Unfortunately Marshal Niel had died, and the portfolio of War went to Le Bœuf, who was vastly inferior. On the whole, the new government was Left Center, or, as Franklin D. Roosevelt put it, "just left of center."

It was, above all, "the Ministry of Good Intentions." Ollivier kept repeating: "We shall give the Emperor a happy old age," and it looked as though all parties concurred in that amiable sentiment. A handful of Legitimists, a small cabal of dictatorial Bonapartists, and a spirited band of radical Republicans stood out. But all the rest united in wishing to give the renovated regime a chance. Ollivier's official receptions at the Place Vendôme were thronged with men who represented all shades of opinion: Prévost-Paradol, a brilliant, scholarly, and redoubtable polemist, was there, as were the venerable fossils of the Louis-Philippe era: Guizot, the impregnable rock of conservatism; Odilon Barrot, once the hesitant leader of the Dynastic Left. The French Academy had kept up a mild, dignified warfare against the regime; it adopted in its turn a policy of appeasement, and elected Émile Ollivier. After three years of bitterness—the winters of our discontent—there was in France a tremulous spring of good will.

Within eight days of its start, that fair promise was nearly destroyed by a stupid accident. Prince Pierre Bonaparte, son of Lucien, had led a life of reckless adventure. A conspirator at fifteen in Italy, a major in the

Colombian army, half insurgent, half bandit in the Maremma, imprisoned in the Castel Sant' Angelo, killing three men in the wilds of Albania, leaving an unsavory reputation in New York and London, he had turned up in France in 1848 as a Red republican. He joined the Foreign Legion, was transferred to the regulars, but for mysterious reasons was cashiered just before the siege of Zaatcha, an Algerian oasis. Napoleon III made him a prince, with a handsome allowance, but kept him at arm's length. Pierre remained tolerably quiet, lived with a workingwoman, honorably married her, and devoted some of his energy to composing mediocre literature. The Reds were viciously attacking the Bonaparte family: out of Corsican clannishness, Pierre engaged in a violent press controversy with Rochefort and Paschal Grousset. The latter sent him his seconds, Ulrich de Fonvielle and Victor Noir. In the course of the discussion, Noir, a mere lad, slapped the prince in the face, and Pierre shot him dead (January 10).

A Bonaparte murdering a republican! What a windfall for the radicals! The funeral of Victor Noir, on January 12, offered a tempting opportunity for an uprising. The government was ready. The ceremony took place at Neuilly, in the west of Paris, miles from the inflammable workingmen's districts. Troops were massed in the Champs-Élysées. The Emperor himself was in uniform, ready to mount his horse. Rochefort, whom chance had turned from a wit to a demagogue, was at any rate no blind fanatic: he refused to unleash an insurrection that would have been crushed in blood. A special court exonerated Pierre on the plea of self-defense, but condemned him to pay heavy damages to the victim's family. Ollivier had handled the situation well; this brief and violent storm did not weaken his government.

Rouher had been relegated to what seemed a gilded sinecure, the Presidency of the Senate. It was he who proposed that the sweeping changes made in the constitution should be submitted to a popular vote. His motives are hard to probe. He was too loyal a Bonapartist (he had remained the personal friend of the imperial family) to wish the government to suffer a defeat, but he was too staunch a conservative to want the liberal trend endorsed by the whole people. The Emperor, whose only thought was for peace and quiet, was dismayed at the risk. But Rouher had good Bonapartist— and Rousseauistic—doctrine on his side: the Social Contract, the Fundamental Pact, should be passed upon by all citizens. Ollivier, as a democrat reconciled with Cæsarism, supported Rouher. The Emperor yielded. Perhaps there was still in him, after so many buffets, some spark of his old faith in his destiny. A plebiscite was ordered: the nation was asked to ratify "the liberal reforms introduced by the Emperor since 1860."

This artful wording produced curious results at both ends of the political line: the Republicans rejected the liberal trend, the authoritarian Bonapartists approved of it. No one was deceived: the actual question was unequivocal: "Do you want Napoleon III to remain on the throne, or do you want a totally new regime?" The men who were most definitely against any kind of plebiscite were the orthodox parliamentarians. They did not like the constant possibility of "a legalized *coup d'état*" superseding their authority, "a trap door that might at any moment spring open under their feet." Daru and Buffet resigned from the cabinet; and Daru, alas, was replaced at the Foreign Office by Gramont.

On May 8, 1870 the plebiscite was taken. Its sincerity never was challenged. Consistently, Paris voted No; and so did the other large cities. But the provinces had shuddered at the progress of the Reds. They rallied overwhelmingly to the Empire. The final count was 7,336,000 for, 1,560,000 against. After twenty-one years at the head of the state, with a new generation of voters, Napoleon III was endorsed by a handsomer majority than he had received on December 10, 1848. The Emperor could tell the future Napoleon IV: "This is your coronation."

On the 25th of May the results were solemnly proclaimed in the Salle des États, part of the vast constructions which, under Napoleon III, finally linked the Louvre and the Tuileries. Few ceremonies under the Empire were so impressive. No one imagined it would be the last. "The Empire is stronger than ever; we are out for another twenty years," Gambetta and Jules Favre somberly acknowledged. The Emperor himself seemed rejuvenated. There was a deep undertone of joy in his firm, even voice. What France had approved was not a mere set of legislative changes, but the very principle of the reign: order as the first condition of liberty and progress. "Between revolution and the Empire, the country has been challenged to choose, and has chosen. . . . My government shall not deviate from the liberal line it has traced for itself. . . . More than ever, we may envisage the future without fear."

CHAPTER NINE

NEMESIS
1870

"MORE than ever, we may envisage the future without fear"—these words of proud serenity were uttered on May 25. On June 30, proposing a reduction of 10,000 in the number of draftees, Émile Ollivier proclaimed: "At no time has peace been more secure." On July 2 came the thunderbolt: the candidacy of a Hohenzollern prince to the uneasy throne of Spain.

In the Franco-German conflict, the responsibility of Bismarck has long been uncontrovertible. We have, not his admission merely, but his gloating revelation of the way in which he trapped France into war. From the nationalistic point of view, he had every reason to act as he did when he did. If France could be branded as the aggressor, the alliance between the German states would come into action, and could easily be turned into a more permanent bond. Conversely, even if France's tentative agreements with Austria and Italy had been more definite, they would have been imperiled or even nullified if France assumed the offensive. Above all, the Prussian army was ready, and the French was not. The opportunity might never occur again. Everything went according to plan. The masterly realism of Bismarck has been admired ever since by all tough-minded historians, whose sole criterion is immediate material success. It gave Europe two generations of cold war, called at that time armed peace, and ultimately two conflagrations that reached the end of the world: for William II and Hitler simply carried out—into disaster—the principles of Bismarck; and these principles have not been fully exorcised from the German mind even today.

But if we must acknowledge the responsibility so proudly assumed by the Iron Chancellor, this does not turn the France of 1870 into an unspotted victim like Belgium in 1914, Denmark or Holland in 1940. Bismarck's deceit was only the bait: the trap was of France's own making. That trap was the old policy of prestige, power, hegemony, leadership, *grandeur*, glory and vainglory: it has many shades and many names. It was at least as ancient as Francis I, and it had twice reached a splendid climax, with Louis XIV and with Napoleon I.

The cause of the quarrel vanished before hostilities broke out, and was soon utterly forgotten. Here are the facts. In 1868 Queen Isabella of Spain, whose policies and private life were equally objectionable, was removed from the throne. Marshal Serrano became regent, Prim head of the ministry. They cast about for a constitutional and liberal sovereign. The Duke of Montpensier, son of Louis-Philippe, was ruled out as unacceptable to Napoleon III. Many candidates were considered; several were approached, and declined. Finally, Prim's choice fell on Prince Leopold of Hohenzollern-Sigmaringen. A chance word of Prim's would seem to indicate that the initiative came from Bismarck.

Europe is sick with ill-digested history; and every nation lives in dread of encirclement. French schoolboys had been taught that the empire of Charles V should never be allowed to rise again, just as British schoolboys were taught that no first-class power should be in control of the Low Countries. When the news of the Hohen-

zollern candidacy reached Paris, the ghost of Charles V
rose menacingly.

It was a very tenuous ghost. John Lemoinne sensibly
pointed out in *Le Journal des Débats* that family considerations were not decisive in international affairs. The
Hohenzollern-Sigmaringen, or Swabian, branch, had
been separated for centuries from the Franconian, later
Prussian, branch. Another Hohenzollern-Sigmaringen
had become Prince of Romania, with the full approval
of Napoleon III. But public opinion did not want to
reason out these dynastic niceties. The mere name Hohenzollern was a red rag to a bull. And the Empire, even
in its authoritarian days, was swayed by public opinion.

What is "the Phantom Public"? Messrs. Malcolm
Carroll and Lynn M. Case have established that France
as a whole was not "grimly determined" to make war.
But it desired a spirited policy: the humiliation of
Sadowa and Luxemburg rankled. To use frankly ana-
chronistic phrases, no more appeasement, not another
Munich! The time had come for a policy of contain-
ment, even of rolling back. The opposition was particularly bellicose. The very men who had proposed the
abolition of standing armies were now clamoring for
a fight. For Jules Favre, this move of Bismarck's was a
casus belli; Gambetta urged all Frenchmen to unite in a
national war; Jules Simon, the quiet, humdrum, smiling
philosopher, wrote that unless France vetoed the candidacy of Prince Leopold, she would forfeit her security
and her dignity. Legitimists, Orléanists, Republicans,
authoritarian Bonapartists, Edmond About, and the
friends of Prince Napoleon, all breathed the same martial ardor. The still small voice of good sense was there,
but it was inaudible. As Francis Magnard wrote in *Le*

Figaro for July 7, "Seldom have we seen such an accord among the organs of the different parties."

The King of Prussia, far wiser than his Chancellor, was averse to war. He would not give his distant cousin any formal order to desist, but he made his desire plain. Prim himself had not intended to start a European crisis: he sent an emissary to Prince Leopold, suggesting that he should withdraw. The Spanish crown was no tempting prize: a few months later, Prim, the king-maker, was assassinated; and Amadeo of Savoy, who accepted the thankless honor of ruling unruly Spain, was to abdicate after two years of misery. Prince Anthony, father of Leopold, announced that the project had been abandoned.

The English press had agreed with the French in considering the whole affair a clumsy provocation on the part of Bismarck. Now the conflict was over: it had been merely a minor flutter, far less threatening to peace than the Luxemburg crisis. Its happy solution was a moral victory for France.

But in Paris the jealous defenders of national prestige were not satisfied. They felt that Bismarck, embittered by his failure, would seek his revenge. He should be defeated decisively, now that they had him on the run. So the French Ambassador to the court of Prussia, Benedetti, was instructed to wait on King William, then at the health resort of Ems, and to request from him a guarantee that he would not permit Leopold to be a candidate again. The King refused to be dragged personally into this quarrel. He had received notification of Leopold's withdrawal, and approved of it. Any further developments would have to be taken through constitutional channels, with the Prussian government in Ber-

lin (July 13). The next day William left Ems. Benedetti went to present his respects at the station; the King
bade him adieu with his wonted courtesy. Thanks to
Benedetti's skill—he had tempered the trenchant demands dictated by Gramont—that new threat to peace
had been averted. It still looked as though "the Trojan
war would not take place."

This would not have suited the war party at Saint-
Cloud and in Paris. It certainly was a bitter disappoint-
ment to Bismarck. He was dining with Moltke and
Roon when he received from his agent Abeken the report of the conversations between the King and Benedetti. He asked Moltke: "Would there be any gain in
postponing the conflict?" The great strategist replied:
"None whatever. It is our interest to hasten it." Thereupon Bismarck touched up the message and made it read,
in substance: "His Majesty has refused to see again the
French Ambassador, and, through the Aide on duty, has
notified him that he had nothing further to say." *Sup-
pressio veri, suggestio falsi:* not quite a forgery, but certainly a moral lie. The doctored text was wired at once
to the Prussian embassies and to the press. That same
night, crowds vociferated in unison, a thousand miles
apart: *"Nach Paris!"* and *"A Berlin!"*

Even at this very last hour, war was not inevitable.
The masses of the French people did not want it; the
Emperor did not want it. Thiers, "as eager as anyone
to obtain reparation for Sadowa," thought the occasion
ill chosen, counseled cool-headedness, demanded com-
munication of the official dispatches. In vain did he
strain his shrill voice: he was hooted down as a traitor.

The man who was technically responsible for the
disastrous turn was the Foreign Secretary, Gramont:

nervous, irritable, insanely proud, he felt that he (and in his own eyes he was France) had received a slap in the face and, as a gentleman, must draw the sword. Had Daru remained at the Foreign Office, common sense might have won a precarious victory. Not for long: Thiers's own words reveal the delusion that made peace such a desperate cause. The Chamber was quasi-unanimous; so was the Paris press; and the Paris mob seemed, by divine right, to voice the will of the nation. Émile Ollivier assented; and he added—words which were to follow him to his grave, forty-three years later: "with a light heart." Napoleon III yielded, with death in his soul.

He was the elect of the deep rural masses, and they wanted peace. Why did he not resume his moral dic-tatorship, curb Parliament, curb the press, curb the mob, as he had done in 1851? Here we find the unanswerable arraignment against all personal regimes. He could not act because he was sick; and a man who assumes the formidable responsibility of dictatorship has no right to be sick. He could not act because he was thinking of the dynasty; and a dictator should have no thought but for his country. Above all, he could not act because peace would have been called "peace at any price," the craven peace of a Louis-Philippe; and he was the heir of the epic military Legend, and he had long basked in its prestige. So phantoms from the past, Louis the Great, Napoleon the Great, arose to strangle the humanitarian ruler who had usurped their trappings.

War was declared on July 19. The alliances were airy castles; the army was a rope of sand; the Emperor was a living corpse.

On the 1st of July, as the Emperor was in great pain,
a consultation was held at the Tuileries. The doctors
were an illustrious group: Nélaton, Ricord, Fauvel, G.
Sée, Corvisart. Their diagnosis, written on July 3, was
fully confirmed by the English specialists who, two years
later, attempted to save Napoleon. Both kidneys and
the bladder were affected; his urine was pus and blood.
The disease went back fully ten years: the autopsy was
to show that the stone had reached enormous propor-
tions. This report was entrusted to Dr. Conneau, Napoleon's intimate friend since the days of Arenenberg.
Through a tragic scruple of "thoughtfulness," he failed
to communicate it to the government and even to the
Empress. Had the truth been known, the course of the
next two weeks might have been different. On the 28th,
Napoleon III and the Prince Imperial left Saint-Cloud
for the front.

The one chance for the French, outnumbered as they
were, was a swift offensive that might throw the pon-
derous Prussian machine off balance. Moltke expected
such an advance and had already marked the point where
it would be checked. The French were denied even such
a brief and illusory success. The first battles—Wissem-
bourg, Wörth, Forbach—were fought on the frontier,
and France was at once invaded. Under the Emperor's
supreme command, the two main armies were entrusted
to Mac-Mahon, Duke of Magenta, and to Bazaine,
whom the opposition, because he was not a favorite at
court, chose to extol and called "our glorious Bazaine."
After the first disastrous shock, Mac-Mahon retreated as
far as Châlons, and Bazaine sought refuge in Metz.

"The Ministry of Good Intentions" was swept away
by this storm. Under the Empress as regent, the direc-

tion of affairs went to General Cousin-Montauban, who was officially known by the title he had won in China, Count Palikao. At Châlons, it was decided that Mac-Mahon would retire farther, so as to cover Paris; the Emperor would at once return to the capital. Whatever the strategic merits of the plan, it was a confession of defeat. So it was vetoed by the Empress and Palikao. Napoleon III should remain with his troops, and march to the relief of Bazaine.

Here we have a very shadowy might-have-been. The events of the next fortnight would seem to indicate that every move would have been futile: the imperial armies were outclassed and already doomed beyond redemption. The detailed story of the campaign by the German General Staff, however, gives a different impression. To quote again Wellington's words after Waterloo, "It was a near thing," much nearer than the ultimate result would show. We must not forget, either, the way in which Gambetta's improvised armies held their own for nearly four months. Had a sounder strategy been adopted, no Valmy, no Miracle of the Marne could have been expected: it was impossible for France to win this hopeless war. But the front could have been stabilized. This achieved, the friendly neutrals, Austria and Italy, might have helped France secure honorable terms.

In his first moves from Châlons, Mac-Mahon had succeeded in eluding the Germans. But, through an indiscretion of the press, his position was revealed, and he had to fall back on Reims. When, in obedience to orders from Paris, he advanced again with Verdun and Metz as his objectives, he was forced northward and all but trapped near the Belgian frontier, at Sedan. There was still a chance of escaping to Mézières. Mac-Mahon, severely wounded, turned his army over to Ducrot. That excellent officer might have saved at least part of his forces. But General de Wimpffen had just arrived from Paris with an order appointing him commander of the army in case Mac-Mahon was disabled. He asserted his right, canceled Ducrot's plan for a retreat, and made a desperate attempt to break through. The hours wasted in this confusion were fatal. The encirclement was now complete. From every height, the German artillery mercilessly pounded the confused masses huddled in the valley. The wild charges of Galliffet were magnificent and futile. Someone had blunder'd.

Wimpffen still refused to understand. He proposed a last effort, which would have been mass suicide. Napoleon III had himself sought death, obstinately: staff officers by his side were killed or wounded. But a soldier's death rejected him. A grand gesture of despair would have been an epic page, somber and splendid, a *Götterdämmerung* that might have remained in the annals of mankind. But Napoleon III felt that he had no right to have brave men massacred for the sake of a prestige in which, in the secret of his heart, he had never fully believed. He resumed command only to surrender. He had the white flag raised and ordered the cease-fire. Eighty thousand men were caught in the net.

A last temptation was before him. For all his resplendent uniforms, Bismarck was first of all a diplomat, not a military man. He would have been glad to stop the campaign and arrange for terms of peace on the battlefield, as Napoleon III had done after Solferino. The terms would have been harsh, for the defeat was unprecedented, but not so crushing as they were to be four months later. If an insurrection broke out in Paris, it

could be quelled by the liberated troops. (Bazaine con-
fusedly entertained a plan of that kind at Metz, and it
explains his prolonged inaction; and it was exactly such
a plan that Thiers, with Mac-Mahon's army, was to
carry out against the Commune.) The regime, although
wounded, would survive. When responsibilities were
investigated, it could easily be proved that they did not
fall on the Emperor alone. Napoleon III brushed aside
the hinted offer. It was his personal sword, not that of
France, that he was giving up to "his brother," the King
of Prussia. He was simply a prisoner of war. His surrender implied total renunciation.

In Paris nothing was known about the situation of the
armies; there even were rumors of a great victory. On
September 2, by six p.m., the facts in their stark horror
reached unofficially, through Brussels, certain members
of the government. On the 3rd the news was spreading,
still uncertain, through the capital. On the 4th the truth
was known at last, and the Empire disappeared.

This, in the eyes of Victor Hugo, was the hour of
expiation he had so long prophesied. France, duped and
enslaved for eighteen years, was set free at last. This interpretation, official in French schools for thirty years or
more, does not tally with the fact that, only four months
before, the country had endorsed the regime by a free
and overwhelming majority. The revolution of the 4th of
September was not purely and simply God's judgment
made manifest through the people's holy wrath. It was a
historical fact, as stupid as most facts, following closely a
well-known pattern, but under unique and tragic circumstances.

The pattern: in 1789, 1792, 1830, 1848, certain

elements in Paris—sincere liberals, professional agitators, the more ardent and the more excitable among the working people—had forced their will upon the capital and upon the nation. The extreme centralization of France, both material and spiritual, created a temptation and a peril: capture Paris, and the whole land is yours. On the 4th of September the mob invaded the Assembly. Under its pressure the Empire was swept away and a provisional government was formed.

It must be noted that this pattern was not invariably successful. Barbès and Blanqui spent their lives starting insurrections that were repressed with ludicrous ease. In June 1848 the movement was formidable, but it failed. In March–May 1871 it was to fail again. An uprising becomes a revolution only when the government in power is weak: blind to realities, infirm of purpose, paralyzed by a bad conscience.

Now, on September 4, the Empire did not move a finger to fight back. The Empress as regent was nominally in control: but the utter vanity of her political role appeared in the hour of peril. She had thought herself determined when she was only willful; she had no popularity and no authority; when she had toyed with power, people shrugged their shoulders. As for Palikao, he was merely an exotic name. In politics and in the army he had been only a secondary character. And he had been at the helm for barely three weeks. Only one man could have rallied the forces of the government: General Trochu, commanding the army of Paris. Trochu was intelligent, well-meaning, not actively disloyal to the regime that had appointed him. He had promised the Empress to die in her defense with the resounding words: "Remember that I am a Breton, a Catholic, and a sol-

dier." But he had a tortuous mind, at the same time hesitant and ambitious. The Paris deputies, who had led
the movement against the Empire, offered him a chance
to head, not a permanent republic, but a government of
National Defense. It seemed the one chance to restore
order, and he accepted.

The essential fact was that the Bonapartists, like all
other Frenchmen, were stunned. This was a paralyzing
blow, worse than Waterloo, worse than Pavia, where
honor at least had been saved. Even Thiers was unable
to see a way out: urged by Mérimée to take action, he
could only wail: "After such a disaster, there is nothing
that can be done." In this moment of utter collapse it
was easy for a determined group to seize power. Their
success is no proof that they represented the nation's will
or the verdict of history.

This is no arraignment of Jules Favre, Gambetta, and
their followers. They were not taking advantage of a
national catastrophe to advance the interests of their
party. They were not defeatists, as the Bolsheviks openly
were in 1917. They had no thought of giving up the
fight: they earnestly believed that the Republic meant
victory. Here we encounter one of those myths which
in history are so much more potent than men of flesh
and blood: the Volunteers of 1792, the Country in
Danger, the rising of all Frenchmen in their might, the
Marseillaise leading the charge, and the despots put to
flight. The men of September 4 did not realize that
1870 was not 1792; that faith may move mountains,
but cannot improvise guns, ammunition, transport, supplies; and that, even in 1792–3, military and diplomatic events were far more confused than they appeared
in the grand saga of the Revolution. These lessons Gam-

betta was to learn in the next four months, at France's
cost; Victor Hugo never learned them at all. I myself
was brought up in republican orthodoxy: sixty years
later, I have come to consider the 4th of September as
a historical accident rather than as a unanimous and final
verdict.

EPILOGUE

REQUIESCANT
1871–1920

ON the 4th of September 1870, Paris was in a mood of elation rather than vindictiveness. However, a mob was massing before the Tuileries, howling: "Down with Badinguet!" (the republicans' name for Napoleon III), and, more ominously: "Death to the Spanish woman!" Eugénie passed through the long and splendid galleries from the Tuileries to the Louvre. Before Perrault's colonnade, an old cab was jogging along. This chance vehicle took the Empress to her American dentist, Dr. Evans. She spent the night at his house. The next day he escorted her to Deauville. A small cutter yacht, *Gazelle*, was in the harbor. The owner, Sir John Burgoyne, gave asylum to the fallen sovereign. The next morning the frail craft sailed through a stormy sea. It was late at night when they reached the Isle of Wight. The small party landed at Ryde. Two days later the Empress met her son at Hastings: he and his tutor Augustin Filon had managed to escape through Belgium.

By September 20 they had settled in their new home, Camden Place, at Chislehurst, a pleasant residential suburb in Kent, some twelve miles from London. Camden Place was no lordly seat, but a large Georgian country house, which the owner, Mr. Strode, had redecorated in French style, with Gobelin tapestries and paneling from the château of Bercy. When he saw it, Admiral Duperré naïvely exclaimed: "Splendid! Looks like a café!"

One political incident marked these first days in England. A busybody, M. Régnier, volunteered to negotiate an agreement between Bazaine, still holding out in Metz, and the Empress. Claiming to each party that he was authorized by the other, he managed to get a number of people involved, including Augustin Filon and General Bourbaki. The Empress brushed the scheme aside. The irrepressible Régnier was later to concoct schemes for a Balkan settlement, and for a reconciliation between Quirinal and Vatican. He ended his imaginative career managing a laundry at Ramsgate.

Meanwhile Napoleon III had been taken to Wilhelmshöhe near Cassel, once a residence of his uncle Jerome, the operetta King of Westphalia. There, on October 30, the Empress visited him. On March 19, 1871 he was liberated, and joined his family at Chislehurst. On March 27 he was invited to Windsor; on April 3 Queen Victoria returned the visit. For two years he was to lead a very quiet life, although not that of a recluse. He could walk, leaning on his wife's arm: suffering had revived and purified the profound affection that the stormy years attacked but could not kill. He read, dabbled in modest experiments, wrote under a pseudonym a pamphlet that passed unnoticed, was working, like Benjamin Franklin, on an economical stove for the poor. Above all, he was perfecting his great project for an International Council, with legislative and judicial power. He was still the man portrayed by Hippolyte Flandrin, peering into the future: peering for his successors, Woodrow Wilson, Franklin Roosevelt, and others still unknown.

But the political embers were warm still, the sense of

a mission had not disappeared; nor the dream of an imperial crown for his son. The final defeat of France had discredited the republicans; the Commune had frightened the bourgeoisie; the ferocity of the repression had seared the soul of the working class; the restoration of the Legitimist pretender was an imminent threat: in every respect, the situation resembled that which followed the days of June 1848, but with more tragic intensity. Once more Cæsarian democracy—order and progress—could be the solution. There were high-placed observers in England and Germany who believed that if France could freely express her choice, she would again endorse the Empire.

Prince Napoleon was ready to work with the Emperor. General Bourbaki, military governor of Lyon, could be trusted. But the Man on Horseback must be able to sit a horse. So Napoleon decided to submit to an operation—lithotrity—fully aware of its dangers at his age and in his condition. It was his last gamble. On January 2, 1873 the first operation was performed; a second followed on the 6th. Both went well. The third was scheduled for the 9th. On the eve, they gave the patient chloral. He slept heavily, barely recovered consciousness, and at eleven a.m. on January 9 he was at peace.

On March 16, 1874 a great rally was held at Chislehurst, to celebrate the coming of age of the Prince Imperial. The general staff of Bonapartism was there, except Prince Napoleon. The young man gave an able speech prepared by Rouher, and he spoke it well, with authority and charm. On June 1, 1879 the prince, a lieutenant in the British forces, was killed in Zululand. Father and son rested at Chislehurst until 1887, when their remains were transferred to Farnborough. The Empress lived to see Sedan avenged by the Treaty of Versailles. She died on July 11, 1920, in the ninety-fifth year of her age.

NOTE ON SOURCES

A MAN who was for twenty-two years the ruler of a great country and who for fifteen appeared as the arbiter of Europe is inevitably the center of an enormous literature. A molehill compared with the paper mountain erected in memory of Napoleon I; still, a molehill that no scholar can hope to conquer even in a long lifetime.

In my *Napoleon III: an Interpretation* (Cambridge, Mass.: Harvard University Press; 1943), an essay in political philosophy rather than a biography, the reader will find a "Bibliographical Essay" (pp. 315–23), which need not be duplicated here. This was intended, not as an exhaustive inventory, but as a guide. It can easily be brought up to date by consulting the various historical reviews. Interest in the Second Empire has not waned in the last decade. Professor Franklin Charles Palm, of the University of California, has been directing research work on the subject for a number of years, and his students have prepared a whole library of monographs, available in typescript. Professor Palm's own contribution is *England and Napoleon III: A Study in the Rise of a Utopian Dictator* (Durham, N. C.: Duke University Press; 1948).

French Opinion on War and Diplomacy during the Second Empire, by Professor Lynn M. Case (Philadelphia: University of Pennsylvania Press; 1954), is of commanding interest. It shows how, in spite of curbs on the press and political meetings, the Second Empire attempted to ascertain public opinion, by methods rather less crude than the modern polls. Professor Lane's previous studies: *Franco-Italian Relations* (*1860–1865*): *The Roman Question and the Convention of September* (Philadelphia: University of Pennsylvania Press; 1932) and *French Opinion on the United States and Mexico, 1860–1867* (New York: D. Appleton-Century Co.; 1936), are also extremely valuable.

Among the best purely biographical monographs in recent years, I should like to mention Ivor Guest: *Napoleon III in England* (London: British Technical & General Press; 1952).

The above will serve as rough indications for the professional student. The general reader who would like further information about the man, the regime, the period, will find a wealth of books available in English. It will be noted that, although the "Black Legend" about Napoleon the Little lingers in the popular mind, all reputable historians in this century are on the whole favorable to that enigmatic character.

GENERAL BACKGROUND: THE PERIOD IN EUROPEAN HISTORY

BINKLEY, ROBERT C.: *Realism and Nationalism, 1852–1871* (The Rise of Modern Europe, edited by William L. Langer, Vol. XVI; New York: Harper & Brothers; 1935). The "Bibliographical Essay," pp. 307–30, is very useful.

GENERAL BACKGROUND: FRENCH HISTORY

AUBRY, OCTAVE: *The Second Empire* (Philadelphia: J. B. Lippincott Co.; 1940). Aubry started in the field of romanced history, and has several books of that ambiguous kind about the Second Empire (*Phantom Emperor; Eugénie, Empress of the French*). But he gradually turned into a very conscientious historian, and his studies of *The King of Rome* and *St. Helena* were based on extremely serious work. The book here listed is packed with encyclopedic information on society and culture as well as politics. A good introduction and a handy reference book.

GUEDALLA, PHILIP: *The Second Empire* (New York: G. P. Putnam's Sons; 1922) is entertaining, and not devoid of historical qualities. Guedalla, although a coruscating wit, was no mere jester. But in order to preserve his lightness of touch, Guedalla chose to ignore the serious aspects of the regime.

BIOGRAPHIES

JERROLD, BLANCHARD: *The Life of Napoleon III.* 4 vols. (London: Longmans, Green & Co.; 1874–82). Partisan; remains valuable for the wealth of documents supplied by the imperial family.

SIMPSON, F. A.: *The Rise of Louis-Napoleon* (London: Longmans, Green & Co.; 1909, 1925). *Louis-Napoleon and the Recovery of France* (London: Longmans, Green & Co.; 1923). Simpson was a pioneer among English scholars in treating Napoleon III with sympathy and respect. Well informed, well composed, well written, in the traditional gentlemanly manner.

D'AUVERGNE, EDMUND B.: *Napoleon III, a Biography* (New York: Dodd, Mead & Co.; 1929). Brief and well-balanced. An unpretentious and excellent introduction.

SENCOURT, ROBERT: *The Life of the Empress Eugenie* (New York: Charles Scribner's Sons; 1931). *Napoleon III, the Modern Emperor* (New York: D. Appleton-Century Co.; 1933). Sencourt, as the "official" biographer of the Empress, had access to many family documents. Valuable and entertaining. Sencourt, however, is frequently careless in details;

206   NOTE ON SOURCES

and his style exaggerates to the point of caricature the Gibbon tradition of courtliness and academic wit.

RHEINHARDT, E. A.: *Napoleon and Eugenie, the Tragicomedy of an Empire,* translated from the German (New York: Alfred A. Knopf; 1931). Readable and dramatic.

JOHN, KATHERINE: *The Prince Imperial* (New York: G. P. Putnam's Sons; 1939).

Great literature is a distorting mirror; mediocrity is frequently more reassuring. However, the works of Victor Hugo and Émile Zola cannot be neglected by any serious student of the Second Empire. Hugo's view of Napoleon the Little became official after Sedan, and remained unchallenged for at least a quarter of a century. It is possible to admire both the genius of the poet and the sincerity of the citizen (in spite of grandiloquent poses and phrases) without accepting his judgment as well-balanced and final. The books that have a bearing on Napoleon III are: *Napoléon le Petit* (1852); *Histoire d'un Crime* (1852, published 1877); *Les Châtiments* (1852 seq.); *L'Année terrible* (1872); *Actes et paroles* (1872 seq.), particularly "*Pendant l'exil*"; *Choses vues* (Vol. I, 1887; Vol. II, 1899), interesting notes on Louis-Napoleon when poet and President were friends; *Les Années funestes* (1897), in the same vein as *Les Châtiments* and *L'Année terrible,* but vastly inferior. These will be found in all the standard editions of Hugo's complete works.

ÉMILE ZOLA: *Les Rougon-Macquart, Histoire naturelle et sociale d'une famille sous le second Empire,* 20 vols., 1871–93. English translation by E. A. Vizetelly, 20 vols., 1885–1907. Apart from his pseudo-scientific claims (for him, a *naturalist* was a *natural scientist*) and from the epic deformation that gives some of his works a weird romantic grandeur, Zola was an actual witness of the age he described, and a gifted as well as a conscientious observer.

ALPHONSE DAUDET's *The Nabob* offers a good picture of imperial Paris, and particularly a searching portrait of Morny.

INDEX

This book was set on the Linotype in a face called *Eldorado*, so named by its designer, WILLIAM ADDISON DWIGGINS, as an echo of Spanish adventures in the Western World. The series of experiments that culminated in this type-face began in 1942; the designer was trying a page more "brunette" than the usual book type. "One wanted a face that should be sturdy, and yet not too mechanical. . . . Another desideratum was that the face should be narrowish, compact, and close fitted, for reasons of economy of materials." The specimen that started Dwiggins on his way was a type design used by the Spanish printer A. de Sancha at Madrid about 1774. Eldorado, however, is in no direct way a copy of that letter, though it does reflect the Madrid specimen in the anatomy of its arches, curves, and junctions. Of special interest in the lower-case letters are the stresses of color in the blunt, sturdy serifs, subtly counterbalanced by the emphatic weight of some of the terminal curves and finials. The roman capitals are relatively open, and winged with liberal serifs and an occasional festive touch.

This book was composed by The Plimpton Press, Norwood, Massachusetts, and printed and bound by The Colonial Press Inc., Clinton, Mass. The typography and binding were designed by the creator of its type-face—W. A. Dwiggins.

WAD